NAFC
Members' Cookbook

Edited by
Mike Vail

North American Fishing Club
Minnetonka, Minnesota

Acknowledgements

We would like to thank the following for their help:

NAFC Members, for sending us those delicious, original wild game recipes that serve as the foundation of the 1997 NAFC Members' Cookbook. These recipes – recommended by your fellow NAFC Members – are certain to delight.

NAFC Staff members, for their diligence, patience and hard work in seeing to the preparation of a useful and readable cookbook of which the NAFC's Members can be proud. They include Book Products Development Manager Steve Perlstein and Book Development Coordinator Dan Kennedy.

Book Design by Zins Design Studio

*Please address reprint requests
and orders for additional cookbooks to:*
NAFC Cookbook Editor
P.O. Box 3401
Minnetonka, MN 55343

ISBN 0-914697-77-3

CONTENTS

Cookbook Abbreviations

tsp. = teaspoon
T. = tablespoon
pt. = pint
oz. = ounce
pkg. = package
qt. = quart

Measurement Conversions

1 pinch = less than ⅛ tsp.
1 T. = 3 tsp.
2 T. = 1 oz.
4 T. = ¼ cup
5 T + 1 tsp. = ⅓ cup
8 T. = ½ cup
16 T. = 1 cup

1 cup = 8 oz.
1 pint = 16 oz.
1 quart = 32 oz.
1 gallon = 128 oz.

1 cup = ½ pint
2 cups = 1 pint
4 cups = 1 quart
2 pints = 1 quart
4 pints = ½ gallon
8 pints = 1 gallon
4 quarts = 1 gallon
8 gallons = 1 bushel

Introduction

Grilling Fish

A. Cort Sinnes

Anyone who's serious about cooking and eating will be quick to tell you that grilling fish is the number one method for cooking fresh fish—preferred above all other cooking methods. Sure, there are plenty of other delicious ways to serve fish, but there's real magic in the combination of something fresh from the water and direct cooking over a live fire. That said, fish is also one of the trickier foods to grill successfully. If you follow the guidelines below, however, you'll be well on your way to grilling any type of fish to perfection, every time you try.

The Best Fish for Grilling

Fish with moderate to high fat content, such as lake trout, salmon, mahi-mahi and tuna, are tops for cooking on the grill. Their natural oils help keep them moist during the hot process of grilling.

Leaner fish, such as perch, rockfish, cod, and snapper, will also cook up beautifully on the grill; they just need a little extra attention to keep them from drying out over the coals.

Some fish, because of their very tender flesh and/or multitude of small bones, are difficult to grill successfully—not impossible, but difficult. These include blackfish, bocaccio, buffalofish, butterfish, California pampano, carp, catfish, Pacific pampano, sablefish and shad.

General Guidelines for Grilling Fish

These guidelines will get you from the grill to the table in fine form:

1 Keep the fish refrigerated until about 30 minutes before grilling. It should near room temperature when it goes on the grill. If the fish is to be marinated for longer than 30 minutes, begin marinating it in the refrigerator and take it out of the refrigerator—but not out of the marinade—about 30 minutes before minutes before grilling.

2 Ignite as many briquettes or as much lump charcoal as it takes to make a bed of coals a little larger in size than the piece of fish you are grilling.

3 Fish will stick to a cold cooking grill, so put the grid over the coals and allow it to become good and hot. Once the grid is hot, use a wire brush to clean it, if necessary. Next, coat the grid with vegetable oil, using a large basting brush, just before you're ready to put on the fish. If the recipe you're using does not call for marinating the fish, by all means, brush the fish itself with a light coating of oil before putting on the cooking grid.

4 Fish should be cooked directly over a hot fire, with the cooking grid 3-5 inches above the coals. If you have a covered grill, cook the fish without putting the cover down. One exception to this rule is a large, whole fish—over 4 pounds—which should be cooked using the indirect method with the cover in place.

Small whole fish—less than 4 pounds—can be cooked directly over the coals, just as you would steaks and fillets. If you're cooking fillets, put them on the grill skin side down first. If the fish are tiny, such as herring, make your life easier by grilling them in a hinged wire basket (which has been oiled lightly or sprayed with a non-stick spray).

5 Years ago, the Canadian Department of Fisheries developed a small pamphlet on cooking fish that has since become a classic. In it, they suggest determining the cooking time for any fish (using any cooking method, including grilling) by simply measuring the fish at its thickest part, and cooking it for 10 minutes per inch of thickness. A 1-inch-thick steak, for example, should take a total of 10 minutes to cook—5 minutes per side.

If you're scrupulous about following this timing method, you'll please everyone—even those who say Americans always overcook fish.

Fish is done when its flesh just begins to flake when probed with a fork. Another way to determine doneness is to peek and see if the flesh is uniformly opaque. Translucent flesh is generally undercooked, though some people prefer it that way—especially with fresh tuna. A large piece of fish or thick steak can also be tested for doneness with an instant-read thermometer. Look for a minimum temperature of 140°.

6 Turn the fish only once; fish just doesn't put up with being messed with on the grill.

7 Almost all types of fish should be served piping hot, if possible, within seconds of coming off the grill. Serve the fish on a platter that has been heated in a warm oven, and if you want everything served hot at the same time, have the rest of your dinner ready to go before putting the fish on the grill.

GRILLED REDFISH FILLETS

4 redfish fillets* (between 6-10 oz. each, depending
   on appetites), approximately 3/4-inch thick
2 T. paprika (mild or hot)
1 tsp. finely ground black pepper
1 tsp. finely ground white pepper
1/2 tsp. cayenne pepper
1 tsp. powdered, dried thyme
1 tsp. powdered, dried oregano
1 tsp. garlic powder
1 tsp. onion powder
2 tsp. salt
6 T. neutral-flavored vegetable oil or melted
   butter or margarine

Start the charcoal (approximately 60 briquettes). Put the cooking grid in place so it has a chance to heat up thoroughly before you grill the fish.

Wash the redfish fillets in cold water and pat dry with paper towels.

Thoroughly mix all the dry spices and herbs together. Pour the mixture on a dinner plate in an even layer. Pour oil or melted butter or margarine on another dinner plate.

When the coals have reached the white-hot stage, arrange them in an even layer with the sides touching. Back in the kitchen, lay the redfish fillets, one at a time, in the dry seasoning mixture, thoroughly coating the fillets on both sides. Next, dip the fillets in the oil or melted butter or margarine and place fillets on a platter, ready for the grill.

Place the redfish fillets directly over the coals and cook approximately 3 minutes. Turn the fillets once and cook for an additional 3-4 minutes. The fish is done when it just begins to flake when probed by a fork.

Serve the grilled redfish fillets with wedges of lemon or lime, your favorite coleslaw, and steamed rice.

*If you aren't fortunate enough to catch a "keeper" redfish that falls inside the parameters of your state's slot limit, or if you don't have access to red drum waters at all, then striped bass, white sea bass, or corbina can be substituted for redfish in this recipe.

RED SNAPPER A LA VERA CRUZ

    3   lbs. red snapper fillets
        light vegetable oil, such as canola
        paprika
        ground white pepper
        chopped fresh cilantro and lemon wedges, for garnish

For the Vera Cruz sauce:

     2   T. vegetable oil
     1   large onion, chopped
     3   garlic cloves, minced
     8   plum tomatoes, peeled, seeded and chopped
    4-6 T. chopped canned jalapeño peppers
    18   pitted green olives, halved
    1/4 tsp. cinnamon
    1/4 tsp. ground cloves
    1/2 tsp. sugar
         Juice of 1/2 lemon
     1   tsp. salt

To make the sauce, heat 2 tablespoons of oil in a medium saucepan. Add the onion and garlic and sauté until the vegetables are soft and transparent, but not browned—about 4 minutes. Add the remaining sauce ingredients and simmer, uncovered, for 5-10 minutes. Remove the pan from the heat and cover it until you are ready to serve the fish.

Start the charcoal (approximately 60 briquettes). Put the cooking grid in place so it has a chance to heat up thoroughly before you grill the fish.

Wash the red snapper fillets in cold water and pat dry with paper towels.

When the coals have reached the white-hot stage and are evenly covered with a fine, white ash, arrange them in an even layer with the sides touching. Back in the kitchen, brush the red snapper fillets with a light coating of vegetable oil and sprinkle fillets with paprika and white pepper. Place fillets on a platter, ready for the grill.

Place the red snapper fillets skin-side-down directly over the coals, and cook approximately 3 minutes. Turn the fillets once, using a thin-bladed spatula, and cook for an additional 3-4 minutes. The fish is done when it just begins to flake when probed with a fork.

While fish cooks, reheat the Vera Cruz sauce.

To serve, arrange the grilled fish fillets on a heated serving platter and top with the sauce. Garnish with chopped fresh cilantro and lemon wedges, if desired.

Shark Steaks with Chili-Lime Butter

    4   shark steaks or pieces, about 1" thick
        vegetable oil
        ground white pepper
        lime wedges and chopped fresh cilantro, for garnish

For the Chili-Lime Butter:
    ¼   cup butter
    3   T. fresh lime juice
    2   tsp. chili powder
    1   tsp. minced lime peel (green part only)
        salt and freshly ground pepper to taste

To make the chili-lime butter, melt the butter in a small saucepan. Remove the butter from the heat and let it cool partially. Add the remaining chili-lime butter ingredients and mix well. Keep the butter warm to use as a sauce at serving time, or let it cool completely, to use as a topping for the hot-off-the-grill shark steaks.

Start the charcoal (approximately 60 briquettes). Put the cooking grid in place so it has a chance to heat up thoroughly before you grill the fish.

Wash the shark steaks in cold water and pat dry with paper towels.

When the coals have reached the white-hot stage, arrange them in an even layer with the sides touching. Back in the kitchen, brush the shark steaks with a light coating of vegetable oil and sprinkle lightly with the white pepper. Place steaks on a platter, ready for the grill.

Place the shark steaks directly over the coals, and cook approximately 5 minutes. Turn the steaks once, using a thin-bladed spatula, and cook for an additional 5 minutes. The fish is done when it just begins to flake when probed with a fork.

To serve, arrange the grilled shark steaks on a heated serving platter and top each steak with a few tablespoons of the chili-lime butter. Garnish with lime wedges and a little chopped fresh cilantro, if desired

NAFC MEMBERS' FAVORITES

MICROWAVED COATED BASS FILLETS

8 bass fillets
   salt
   pepper
1/2 lemon
1 cup coat-and-bake seasoning mix for pork
1 cup coat-and-bake seasoning mix for chicken

Salt and pepper the fish to taste and squeeze a small amount of lemon juice on each side. Combine the seasoning mixes and place them in a pie plate. Roll the fillets in this mixture. Place fillets on second pie plate, and microwave on high 3-4 minutes, turning the plate once. Turn the fillets over and microwave 4 more minutes or until the fillets become flaky.

Ralph Branham
Canton, North Carolina

BASS TO DIE FOR

1-2 lbs. bass fillets
    melted butter or margarine
1   can cream of mushroom soup
1/3 cup white wine
1/4 cup diced onion
    seasonings to taste (salt, pepper and herbs)

Dip the fillets in melted butter. Roll up fillets and secure each with a toothpick. Mix the remaining ingredients together in a bowl. Place the fillets in a baking dish and pour soup mixture over the fillets. Bake at 350° for 30 minutes, turning fillets once and ladling sauce over them

This recipe is also good with other white fish.

Donald Propst
Charlotte, North Carolina

Richard Hoag

ITALIAN STYLE STRIPER FILLETS

	Striped bass fillets	soda crackers,crushed
	water	Italian seasoning
1	T. baking soda	garlic salt
2	eggs	oil for frying
½	cup milk	

Soak the fish for ½ hour in enough water to cover mixed with baking soda. Rinse the fish and then pat dry. Beat the eggs with the milk. Crush the soda crackers very fine with a rolling pin. Dip the fish first in the egg and milk and then with cracker crumbs. Sprinkle fillets with Italian seasoning and the garlic salt. Brown fillets in skillet in hot oil until done, turning once.

Richard Hoag
Lake Havashu, Arizona

GRILLED BASS FILLETS

bass fillets
butter
mayonnaise
paprika
sweet onion, sliced
minced garlic
lemon wedges

Place fillets on a sheet of aluminum foil that has been rubbed with butter. Brush fillets lightly with mayonnaise and sprinkle with paprika. Place a few slices of sweet onion and some minced garlic on each fillet. Wrap foil around fillets to make a loose package. Grill over direct heat for 5 minutes, then turn package over and cook for 3 more minutes. Remove and serve with lemon wedges.

Bill Parmenter
Coventry, Rhode Island

BASS BARBECUE

8 bass fillets
1 tsp. salt
1/4 tsp. pepper
1/4 tsp. paprika
8 slices of bacon, divided
2 T. lemon juice, divided

Sprinkle fillets with salt, pepper and paprika, and set aside. Put two slices of bacon on a large piece of aluminum foil. Place two fillets lengthwise on each bacon slice and sprinkle with ½ teaspoon lemon juice. Repeat to make
3 more packets. Grill packets over hot coals for 10 minutes; turn packets over and grill another 10 minutes or until fish flakes.

Daryl Hoffmann
Harvey, North Dakota

FRIED CALICO BASS

boneless calico bass fillets
egg
flour
oil for frying
spices and herbs of your choice
lemon juice

Rinse the fillets in cold water and dip in beaten egg and then flour. Fry in skillet in hot oil 3-4 minutes per side. Sprinkle fillets with spices and herbs to taste, and add a spritz of lemon juice.

Calico bass has a rich flavorful taste to it; and it's good eating.

Bryan M. Bartlett
Chula Vista, California

GRILLED BASS WITH TOMATO SAUCE

4   large bass fillets, cleaned and boned
2   celery stalks, finely chopped
2   cans of tomato sauce
1   tsp. garlic powder
¼   tsp. hot pepper sauce
2   T. lemon pepper
    salt
    pepper
1   lemon, sliced

Prepare the grill for medium direct heat. Mix celery, tomato sauce, garlic powder, hot pepper sauce, and lemon pepper in a medium saucepan. Stir and let simmer for 3-4 minutes. Season the fillets with salt and pepper and wrap in foil that has been sprayed with non-stick spray. Grill for 4-5 minutes. Open foil and spoon the tomato sauce over the fillets. Cook 10-15 minutes more. Remove fillets from foil and garnish with lemon slices.

Jonathan Fulliloue
Indianola, Mississippi

BASS AND RICE

2-5 lbs. bass fillets
cooked rice
1 onion, sliced
salt
pepper
garlic salt
½ cup butter

Place about half the cooked rice in a casserole dish and top with half of bass fillets and half of onion slices. Sprinkle with salt, pepper and garlic salt. Repeat with second layer of each. Melt the butter and pour over fish. Cover with foil; bake for 1 hour at 350°.

Derek Spradlin
North Little Rock, Arkansas

BASS ROMANOFF

8 large- or smallmouth bass fillets
2 large white onions, chopped
1 clove garlic, minced
2 T. olive oil
1 lb. fresh mushrooms, chopped
3 cups sour cream
2 limes
1 lemon, cut into wedges

Preheat oven to 350°. In a large skillet, sauté onions and garlic in oil on high for 3 minutes. Add mushrooms and sauté 3 more minutes. Spoon onion and mushroom mixture into a large bowl and add sour cream and the juice from the limes.

Arrange the bass fillets in a large, deep baking pan. Pour sour cream mixture over fish; bake for 20 minutes, or until fish flakes away. Serve with lemon wedges.

Brad Sime
Merrillville, Indiana

GRILLED BASS IN FOIL

2 large bass fillets (about 14 " long)
 juice of 2 lemons
2 tsp. pepper
2 T. butter, melted
3 green onions, finely chopped

Cut enough foil to fold up and loosely cover the fish. Fold up all sides of the foil to create 6 inch sides. Cover the bottom of foil dish with ¼ inch water. Place the fillets in the water and add the lemon juice. Sprinkle pepper evenly over fillets. Place chopped green onions in the water around fillets. Fold the sides of the foil down over fillets, pinching to seal; place on grill. Cook for 15-25 minutes, or until fish flakes. Take off grill and serve.

Tim Vann
LaPorte, Indiana

BEER BREADED BASS

boneless bass fillets	³/₄ cup beer
crackers, finely ground	¼ cup milk
seasoning salt	2 eggs, beaten
sugar	flour
	oil for frying

Place crackers into a bowl; add a few shakes of seasoning salt and sugar. In another bowl, mix the beer, milk and eggs. Coat fillets with flour and dip into the egg mixture; then coat with the cracker mixture. Drop fillets into a preheated deep-fat fryer and cook until golden brown. Drain on paper towels until cool enough to eat.

Arthur Sweatt
Laconia, New Hampshire

FRESH AND SALT-WATER COMBO

- 1 lb. bass fillets
- 1 tsp. salt
- ½ cup thinly sliced mushrooms
- 1 T. butter
- 1 cup dry sherry
- 2 tsp. minced (instant) onion
- ⅓ cup water
- 1 T. cornstarch
- 2 T. lemon juice
- 1 T. snipped parsley
- 7 oz. cleaned raw shrimp, fresh or frozen

Divide fillets into 4 portions and sprinkle each with ¼ teaspoon salt. Cook the mushrooms in butter until tender but not brown. Stir in the sherry and onion. Mix the water and cornstarch until smooth; stir into the mushroom mixture. Cook, stirring constantly, until the mixture thickens and boils. Boil and stir for 1 minute. Stir in lemon juice and parsley. Remove from heat.

Place 1 portion of fish on each of four 14 x 9 inch pieces of double-thickness aluminum foil. Top fish portions evenly with shrimp. Turn up edges of the foil and spoon the mushroom sauce evenly over the shrimp. Wrap the fish securely in the foil and place the packets on a grill, 4 inches from medium coals. Cook for 20-25 minutes or until the fish flakes easily with a fork. If you are baking, cook in a 400° oven.

William J. Wallace
Conyers, Georgia

GRILLED STRIPED BASS

2	lbs. striped bass steaks (about 6 steaks)
1/2	cup butter, melted
1/3	cup sherry
1/3	cup lemon juice
1	clove garlic, minced
2	T. soy sauce
2	T. chopped fresh dill weed
1	tsp. salt
2	T. butter, melted

Place steaks in a large shallow container. Mix remaining ingredients, except the 2 tablespoons melted butter. Pour mixture over fish and refrigerate for 30-45 minutes, turning fish once.

Remove fish from the marinade, reserving the marinade. Grill steaks directly over hot coals for 8-10 minutes per side, or until the fish flakes, brushing steaks often with the marinade.

Daryl Hoffmann
Harvey, North Dakota

STRIPED BASS FILLETS WITH GINGER VINAIGRETTE

- 4 striped bass fillets
- 1 cup extra virgin olive oil
- ¼ cup red wine vinegar
- 2 large shallots, minced
  juice of 2 limes
- 2 T. soy sauce
  1" piece of ginger, peeled and minced
- 2 T. dark sesame oil
  salt
  pepper
- 1 bunch of fresh parsley, chopped
- ¼ cup toasted sesame seeds

In a mixing bowl, combine the olive oil, vinegar, shallots, lime juice, soy sauce and ginger. Stirring vigorously, add the sesame oil, salt,and pepper to taste.

Season the striped bass on both sides with salt and pepper. Grill fillets, skin-side down, over high heat until lightly done, or sauté the fillets in a little butter or oil. (Note: Striped bass fillets that are ½ inch thick take only 1-2 minutes per side to cook.)

Just before serving, stir the parsley into the vinaigrette.

Serve fillets with steamed rice. Top rice with the fish and drizzle vinaigrette sauce over top. Garnish with toasted sesame seeds and parsley.

Ray Saldi
Voorhees, New Jersey

CHICO'S BASS FILLETS

6-8 bass fillets
1 qt. buttermilk
1 large yellow onion
1 large red pepper
½ cup red wine
garlic salt (or seasoning salt of your choice)
pepper
butter

Place the bass fillets in a shallow cake pan and cover with buttermilk. Place in the refrigerator, uncovered, for at least 1 hour (this will firm up the bass fillets). Drain and rinse the fillets and place them on a nonstick baking sheet with edges.

Slice the onion and red pepper into thick rings and place on top of the fillets. Splash red wine over the fillets. Sprinkle with garlic salt and pepper. Top each fillet with a small piece of butter. Bake at 325° until the onions are brown and the fillets flake with a fork.

Rick Bowman
Racine, Wisconsin

STRIPED BASS BREADING

striped bass fillets
2 cups finely crushed
soda crackers
½ tsp. garlic powder
¼ tsp. black pepper
¼ tsp. salt
2 T. milk
1 egg
oil for frying

In shallow dish, combine crackers, garlic powder, pepper and salt. Beat the milk and egg together in bowl. Dip the fillets in the milk and egg mixture, then roll in the cracker breading. Deep fry fillets until golden brown.

Larry Montle
Montrose, Michigan

POND POINT STRIPER WITH PENNE

4 lbs. striped bass fillets
3 oz. sundried tomatoes
2 dozen shrimp, peeled and deveined
½ cup butter
  freshly ground black pepper
1½ lbs. uncooked penne pasta
¼ cup olive oil
12 whole cloves garlic, peeled
1 T. capers, drained
⅓ cup dry white wine
1 avocado, cubed

Preheat the oven to 400° and start 6 quarts of water boiling for the pasta. Soak the tomatoes in 2 cups of hot water for about 15 minutes. Place the fillets evenly on 4 large pieces of foil; top with shrimp, some dots of butter and a dash of black pepper; seal foil packets and place in the oven for 18-25 minutes.

Cook the pasta just until tender. Meanwhile, in a skillet, heat the oil and any remaining butter over medium-low. Add the garlic cloves, cover and cook until soft and lightly browned, stirring occasionally. Drain the tomatoes, pat dry, and add to the skillet along with the capers. Increase the heat under the skillet and cook 2 minutes, stirring constantly. Add the wine and simmer for 1 minute.

Drain the pasta well and place in a large serving platter. Unwrap the fish and place fillets over the pasta along with any liquid from the packets. Sprinkle the cubed avocado over the pasta and spoon the contents of the skillet over top. Serve at once with salad, hot bread and white wine. Crushed red pepper flakes can be sprinkled over individual portions if anyone likes a spicier taste.

Richard Zablauskas
Bronx, New York

BROILED FILLET OF FISH

  bass fillets
½ cup melted butter
¼ cup lemon juice
  salt
  pepper
½ tsp. chopped parsley
  paprika

Place the fillets on the broiler rack or on foil. Baste with the melted butter and lemon juice. Broil for 10 minutes. Turn fillets over and baste again. Continue broiling until fish flakes with a fork. Sprinkle with parsley, paprika, salt, and pepper to taste. Serve fillets with melted butter or lemon butter.

Ron and Becky Zirkel
Medora, Indiana

BATTER-DIPPED BLACKFISH

4 blackfish or walleye fillets, (about 1 lb.)
1 cup flour
1½ cups milk
1 T. garlic powder
1 T. onion powder
1 T. dried marjoram
1 pinch salt
1 pinch black pepper
1 pinch ground ginger
¼ cup extra virgin olive oil

Combine all ingredients except fish and oil, to make a thick batter. Dip the fillets in the batter. Fry in skillet in hot oil over medium to medium-high heat until golden brown on both sides. Serve hot.

Ronald Meltreder
Freehold, New Jersey

BLUEFISH "FAUTSUNOD"

2-3 lbs. bluefish fillets
2 cups white wine
   juice of 2 lemons
1 tsp. Worcestershire
   sauce
1 T. seafood
   seasoning
1 tsp. cayenne
   pepper
1 tsp. salt
2 medium onions,
   chopped
3 slices uncooked
   bacon, chopped

Joseph J. Pipon III

In a large bowl, combine the wine, lemon juice, Worcestershire sauce, seafood seasoning, cayenne, and salt. Place the fillets in the mixture and marinate for 20-30 minutes at room temperature. Remove the fillets from the marinade and place in a baking dish with the marinade poured over. Sprinkle the onions and bacon on top of the fillets. Broil for 10 minutes or until bacon is crisp. Finish by baking at 350° for 3-4 minutes or until fish flakes. Serve with white rice.

Joseph J. Pipon III
Budd Lake, New Jersey

BAKED BLUEFISH AND SHRIMP

2-3 bluefish fillets (or any other strong-flavored fish,
     such as mackerel)
1 green pepper, diced
2 cloves garlic, minced
1 T. olive oil
1 14½-oz. can of stewed tomatoes
1 tsp. red wine vinegar
1 tsp. Dijon mustard
    dash of white pepper
¼ tsp. ground coriander
    (kills the strong bluefish flavor)
½ tsp. dried oregano
½ tsp. dried basil
    freshly ground black pepper or 3-4 drops of hot
     pepper sauce (optional)
3-4 plum tomatoes, sliced
½ lb. defrosted popcorn shrimp or calico scallops

Preheat the oven to 400°. Sauté the green pepper and the garlic in the olive oil for 3-5 minutes. In a medium bowl, mix the stewed tomatoes, red wine vinegar, mustard, white pepper and coriander. Add the sautéed peppers and garlic to the bowl and mix thoroughly.

Grease a glass baking dish with butter and arrange the fillets in it. Pour the tomato mixture over the fillets and sprinkle the oregano and basil over top. If you like it spicy, add the black pepper or the hot pepper sauce. Bake the fillets for 15-20 minutes.

Remove the fillets from the oven and top with the plum tomatoes and the shrimp or scallops. Return the dish to the oven and bake an additional 10-15 minutes, or until the shrimp turn pink or the scallops are firm and opaque.

Serve with a mixture of long-grain white and wild rice, or pasta, and a green salad.

Richard Deptula
Commack, New York

SURFCASTER'S BLUES

4	bluefish fillets with skin	½	cup mayonnaise
3	oz. sundried tomatoes	1	tsp. chili powder
4	oz. roasted red peppers	½	tsp. curry powder
2	cloves garlic, crushed		ground black pepper
1	small red onion		non-stick cooking spray
	chopped	2	tsp capers

Soak tomatoes in hot water for about 15 minutes. Drain and save liquid. Place tomatoes, peppers, garlic, onion, mayonnaise and spices, into a food processor. Pulse chop until coarsely blended. Add reserved tomato liquid as needed to bring mixture to the consistency of a cream.

Line a broiler pan with foil and spray lightly with cooking spray. Place fillets on foil, skin-side-down. Add capers to sauce and spoon over fillets. Place under broiler, about 10-12 inches from the heating element. The fish will be done when the top has browned. Serve with salad, hot bread and wine.

Richard Zablauskas
Bronx, New York

BROILED BLUEFISH

bluefish fillets (including the dark meat)
salt
pepper
onion, sliced
mayonnaise

Season the filleted bluefish with salt and pepper or your favorite seafood seasoning. Lay some slices of onion over the fish and cover with a generous layer of mayonnaise (¼ inch thick). Put the fish under the broiler, or bake until the meat is white and flaky.

John H. Hymon
Richmond, Virginia

BLUEGILL POPCORN

1	lb. bluegill fillets, boned and diced
2	eggs, beaten
2	cups beer
1	cup flour
1	cup yellow cornmeal
1/8	tsp. black pepper
1/8	tsp. salt
1/8	tsp. red pepper
1/4	tsp. Cajun spicy shrimp seasonings
2	cups olive oil for deep frying

Mix the eggs with the beer. Marinate the diced fillets in the egg and beer mixture for 5-10 minutes in the refrigerator. Mix the flour, cornmeal and spices. Remove diced fillets from egg and beer mixture, using a slotted spoon, then roll the fillets in the flour mix. Fry the fillets for 5-8 minutes in a deep fryer.

Douglas Sanders
Sarcoxie, Missouri

CARP

FISH CAKES

1 pint canned fish with liquid (we use canned carp
   and suckers that we get during the jigging
   season)
1 egg
   dash of black pepper
¼ lb. crackers, crushed fine
   oil for frying

Combine the fish, egg, and pepper. Add all but ½ cup of cracker crumbs. Mix well and form into patties. Roll the patties in the remaining cracker crumbs. Fry in skillet in ¼ inch of hot oil until both sides are brown. Serve hot.

Leonard Mincks
Halfway, Missouri

BEER BATTERED CARP

2 lbs. carp fillets
¾ cup pancake mix
¼ cup yellow cornmeal
1 tsp. salt
½ tsp. paprika
1 can of beer
1 egg
   oil for frying

Mix all dry ingredients together, then add beer and egg. Mix well. Batter will be medium thick. Coat fish with batter. Deep-fry fish until browned.

Lewis Drullinger and Jody Brown
Woodstock, Kansas

CAJUN CATFISH COURT-BOULLION

4-5 lbs. catfish (or any lean white flesh fish),
    cut into 2" pieces
    cayenne pepper, salt, black pepper, or your
    favorite seasoning salt
  3 T. vegetable or peanut oil
  1 small onion, chopped
  2 cloves garlic, minced
 1/2 bunch fresh parsley, chopped
  3 single stalks celery, chopped
  1 large red bell pepper, chopped
  1 large bunch of green onions, chopped
 1 1/2 T. flour
  2 large cans tomato sauce
 1/2 tsp. thyme
 1/2 tsp. oregano
 1 1/2 large bay leaves
 1/2 cup water
    juice from 1/2 lemon or 4 thin slices

For this recipe, you will need a large, heavy duty aluminum or cast iron.
Dutch oven with a snug fitting lid. Select 1 you can handle easily to
shake, as you should never stir the fish while cooking.

Rub the pieces of your fish well with salt and pepper, or seasoning salt.
Put oil in the cold pot and arrange a layer of fish on the bottom. After
chopping all of the vegetables, including the parsley, sprinkle generously
over the fish. Then sprinkle 1 T. of flour over the vegetables, and add half
the tomato sauce. Repeat with another layer of fish, vegetables, flour,
and remaining tomato sauce. Add the thyme, oregano, bay leaves,
water, and lemon.

Place the pot on very low heat and cook slowly for approximately
1 hour or until tender. Shake the pot often and never stir, to avoid
breaking up the fish. After it is done, top off with seasonings to
taste and serve over rice.

Perry E. Pittman, Sr.
Plano, Texas

CATFISH AND SLAW SANDWICHES

2	4-oz. farm-raised catfish fillets
1	cup thinly sliced green cabbage
3	T. minced radish
1	T. plain nonfat yogurt
1	T. reduced-calorie mayonnaise
½	tsp. paprika
¼	tsp. garlic powder
¼	tsp. pepper
	cooking spray
2	kaiser rolls, split

Combine the cabbage, radish, yogurt and mayonnaise in a bowl; stir well and set aside. Combine the paprika, garlic powder and pepper, and sprinkle over both sides of the fillets. Place the fish on a broiler rack coated with cooking spray and broil 4 inches from the heat source for 4 minutes. Turn the fillets and broil an additional 4 minutes or until fish flakes easily when tested with a fork.

Spoon half of the cabbage mixture onto each kaiser roll; top with the filet.

Goes great with fresh fruit and sparkling mineral water.

Leo G. J. Seffelaar
Broadview, Saskatchewan

CRISP FRIED CATFISH

- 2 lbs. catfish fillets
- 3 cups vegetable oil (for deep frying)
- 1 unripe mango, peeled, seeded and shredded
- 8 medium garlic cloves, thinly sliced and fried in
    1 T. vegetable oil until crisp
- 1 piece fresh ginger, minced or finely shredded
- 2 T. sugar
- 2 T. fish sauce
   fresh lime juice
- 2 red serrano chilies, seeded and slivered
- 1 T. chopped fresh cilantro leaves

Fit a steamer rack inside a large saucepan. Add water to just below the rack and bring to a rapid boil over high heat. Steam the fish fillets until opaque and just tender, about 8-10 minutes. Let the fish cool.

Heat the oil in a wok or deep-fryer to 375°. Pat the fish dry and remove any bones. Cut the fish into bite-size pieces; add to the wok in batches and fry until crisp and well browned. Remove the catfish with a slotted spoon and drain thoroughly on paper towels.

Mix the mango, garlic, and ginger in a small bowl. Mound mixture in the center of a serving platter; surround with the fried fish. Combine the sugar, fish sauce and lime juice in a cup and stir until the sugar dissolves. Sprinkle most of the sauce over the mango mixture. Sprinkle the remaining sauce over the fish.

Garnish with the chilies and cilantro. Serve immediately.

Peter Wells
Quincy, Massachusetts

SUSIE'S BAKED CATFISH DIJON

2   lbs. catfish fillets
    salt
    pepper
$^3/_4$ cup thinly sliced
     onion
2   T. butter
1   cup mayonnaise
$^1/_4$ cup Dijon mustard
2   T. dry vermouth
$^1/_2$ T. hot pepper sauce
$^1/_4$ cup chopped fresh
     parsley
    lemon wedges

Preheat the oven to 350°. Arrange the fish in a shallow baking dish, and add salt and pepper to taste. Top with the sliced onion and dot with butter. Bake 20 minutes or until the fish flakes easily.

Brad Dickerson

Mix the mayonnaise, mustard, vermouth and hot pepper sauce together. Pour over the fish, and broil 2-3 minutes, until brown and bubbly. Sprinkle parsley over the top of finished dish. Serve hot with lemon wedges.

Wayne and Susie Dickerson
Bushnell, Florida

CATFISH CREOLE

- 1 lb. catfish fillets
- 1/3 cup oil
- 1/4 cup flour
- 1/2 cup water
- 1 cup sliced celery
- 1/2 cup sliced green onions, including the green part
- 1/2 cup chopped green pepper
- 2 cloves garlic, crushed
- 1 small can whole tomatoes, cut into small pieces
- 1 8 oz. can tomato paste
- 1 1/2 tsp. salt
- 2 bay leaves
- 1/2 tsp. pepper
- 1 T. brown sugar
- 1 T. lemon juice
- 1 tsp. Worcestershire sauce
- 2 dashes hot pepper sauce
- 1/4 cup chopped fresh parsley
  hot cooked rice

Cut the fillets into 1 inch pieces. Heat the oil in a large pan. (I use an electric skillet.) Add the flour and stir until brown. Remove from the heat and cool slightly. Add the water gradually, stirring until blended. Add all of the remaining ingredients, except the fish and the rice.

Cover and simmer for 20 minutes, or until the vegetables are tender. Remove the bay leaves and add the catfish. Simmer for 8-10 minutes more or until the fish flakes when touched with a fork. Serve over rice in soup bowls.

Bill James
Tooele, Utah

SOUR CREAM BAKED CATFISH

12 catfish fillets
1/2 cup mayonnaise
1 1/2 T. flour
2 cups sour cream
3 T. chopped stuffed
   green olives
1 tsp. celery salt
1/2 tsp. pepper
1/2 tsp. paprika
1/4 tsp. dried thyme
1 T. chopped fresh
   dill weed, or 1 tsp.
   dried dill weed
   lemon wedges and
   parsley sprigs

Place fillets in a well-greased baking pan. Combine the mayonnaise and flour. Add the sour cream, olives, celery salt, pepper, paprika and thyme. Spread the sauce over the fish and then sprinkle with the dill weed. Bake in a 350° oven for 25 minutes, or until the fish flakes easily when touched with a fork.

Garnish the plate with lemon wedges and parsley sprigs and serve.

Bill James
Tooele, Utah

DEEP-FRIED CAJUN CATFISH

1-2 lbs. catfish fillets
1 cup lemon juice
1 1/2 cups yellow cornmeal
1/2 cup flour
2 T. Cajun spice
1 T. salt
1/2 tsp. black pepper
1/2 tsp. red pepper
1/2 tsp. chili powder
   oil for frying

Cut the catfish into finger-size strips and marinate in the lemon juice for 5-10 minutes. Mix the cornmeal, flour and spices in a medium bowl. Roll the catfish strips in this mixture. Let them stand for 2-3 minutes, then roll again. Deep fry strips in 350° oil for 3-4 minutes or until golden brown.

James Carpenter
Lexington, Indiana

CREOLE CATFISH

2-3	lbs. catfish fillets	1	tsp. dried basil
1½	cups chopped tomatoes		leaves
½	cup chopped green pepper	¼	tsp. coarse ground
⅓	cup lemon juice		black pepper
1	T. salad oil	4	drops of hot pepper
2	tsp. salt		sauce
2	tsp. minced		tomato wedges
	instant onions		green pepper rings

Heat the oven to 500°. Place the fillets in a greased 9 x 13 inch pan. Combine the remaining ingredients, except tomato wedges and green pepper rings and spoon over the fillets. Bake for 8-10 minutes, or until the fish flakes easily. Garnish with the tomato wedges and green pepper rings.

David Stokes
Duluth, Minnesota

LOW-FAT OVEN FRIED CATFISH

6	medium-size catfish fillets	2	cups crushed
	salt		cornflakes
	lemon juice		seafood seasoning
½	cup water		vegetable oil spray
½	cup fat-free evaporated		
	milk		

Rinse fillets with water. Put catfish fillets into ice-cold water; add salt and lemon juice and let soak for ½ hour.

Mix ½ cup water and evaporated milk together in a bowl. Place cornflakes in shallow dish. Remove fillets from water, pat dry, and dip into milk mixture. Roll fillets in cornflakes and season with seafood seasoning.

Place fillets on a rack in a pan or on a broiler pan that has been sprayed with non-fat vegetable spray. Bake at 500° for 20 minutes, or until the fish flakes.

Bill Blinkwolt
Oak Forest, Illinois

SPICY CATFISH BROIL

    catfish fillets
1/4 cup butter or margarine
  3 T. lemon juice
1 1/2 tsp. Creole seasoning
1/2 cup whole or sliced almonds

Combine butter or margarine and lemon juice. Dip each fillet in lemon juice mixture. Arrange fillets in 13 x 9 inch. baking dish, and pour remaining lemon juice mixture over fish. Sprinkle fish with Creole seasoning and almonds. Bake at 375° for 25-30 minutes.

Otis McNeal
Mt. Vernon, Georgia

CATFISH BATTER

    catfish
1/2 cup cornmeal
  1 cup self-rising flour
  2 eggs
1/2 tsp. garlic salt
1/2 tsp. onion powder
1/2 tsp. black pepper
    milk
    oil for frying

Filet or cut the catfish into chunks. Mix the cornmeal, flour, eggs, garlic salt, onion powder and black pepper. Add milk to achieve desired consistency. Dip the fillets or fish nuggets in the batter, and deep-fry or pan fry until golden brown.

William E. Hux
Bullhead City, Arizona

BLACKENED CATFISH

catfish fillets, no thicker than ³/₄ "
unsalted butter, melted

Blackened seasonings:	Butter sauce:
1¹/₂ tsp. salt	¹/₂ cup unsalted butter, melted
1 T. paprika	
1 tsp. onion powder	1 T. fresh squeezed lemon juice
1 tsp. garlic powder	
1 tsp. dried thyme	1 green onion, finely minced
¹/₂ tsp. dried oregano	
¹/₂ tsp. black pepper	¹/₄ tsp. cayenne
1 tsp. cayenne	¹/₄ tsp. salt

Mix the blackened seasonings together. Heat the butter for the butter sauce, add remaining sauce ingredients, and keep warm while you prepare the fish. Dip the fish fillets in the plain melted butter. Lay fillets on wax paper, and the butter will harden onto the cold fillets. Sprinkle the seasoning mix on both sides of fillets and pat it into the butter.

Put a cast-iron skillet over high heat until the pan begins to smoke and white ash forms on the bottom, at least 10 minutes. Sprinkle a few drops of water in the pan. If they dance, the skillet is hot enough. Put the seasoned coated fillets in the skillet and cook until the bottoms are blackened, up to 2 minutes. Serve with the butter sauce.

Note: You need a very hot cast-iron skillet. I do this outside on a propane camp stove, a barbecue grill isn't hot enough. You can do it inside, but you better have the exhaust fan on and the windows open in the kitchen for good ventilation.

V. Leon Joyce
Sterling, Virginia

STIR-FRY CATFISH WITH VEGETABLES

1	lb. catfish (or other fish)	1	lb. snow peas
1	T. cornstarch	1/2	cup shiitake
6	T. stir-fry sauce		mushrooms, sliced
1/2	cup vegetable oil	1	T. vegetable oil
	dash of garlic		mixed with 1/4
	dash of ginger		cup water

Bone the catfish and slice it into strips about the size of the pea pods. Mix the strips with the cornstarch and the stir-fry sauce. Cook in skillet at medium-high heat 3-4 minutes with 1/2 cup garlic and ginger, stirring carefully.

Remove the fish strips from the pan and add the snow peas, mushrooms, and oil and water mixture. Cook 5-10 minutes, depending on the crispness desired in pea pods. Return the catfish to the pan and stir until hot.

Chuck Cooley
Allegan, Michigan

HOWDY-CATFISH FILLETS

	catfish fillets	1	tsp. paprika
2	cups buttermilk	1	tsp. salt
1	cup yellow cornmeal	1	tsp. black pepper
1/2	cup flour		lard for frying

Soak your catfish fillets in a large bowl in the buttermilk for 2 hours. Roll the fillets in a mixture of the remaining ingredients, except the lard. Cook the fish in lard in a cast-iron skillet until done and brown.

While your grease is hot, cook some hush puppies and fried taters, too.

Norman E. Jones, Jr.
Marietta, Georgia

SOUR CATFISH

    5   lbs. catfish
    4   cups water
    4   bay leaves
    2   cloves
    2   cups vinegar
   10   allspice berries
    1   tsp. sugar
    1   large onion, sliced
   10   whole peppers
        salt, to taste

Pour boiling water over the fish. Dress fish, removing the skin and head. Cut the fish into 1 inch slices. In large pot, combine water and the remaining ingredients, except gravy. Bring to a boil over high heat. When the water is boiling, put the fish in for 8 minutes, or until the meat comes off the bone. Then it is done. Remove fish from water. Pour gravy over the fish and chill. When it is cold, the gravy gets like jelly and the fish is ready to serve.

Jerry Solberg
Weyauwega, Wisconsin

CHANNEL CATFISH SAUTÉ

        catfish, cut into pieces
   ½   cup flour
   ½   cup yellow cornmeal
    1   tsp. salt
    1   tsp. pepper or lemon pepper
        vegetable shortening or oil

In shallow dish, combine flour, cornmeal, salt and pepper. Dredge catfish pieces in mixture, and fry in shortening or oil until done. Do not overcook.

Jerry Solberg
Weyauwega, Wisconsin

APPLE CIDER CATFISH

  1   whole, dressed catfish (2-4 lbs.)
  2   cups apple juice or apple cider
  1   cup lemon-lime soda
 1/4 cup Worcestershire sauce
 1/4 cup white wine
  3   T. dried oregano, crushed and rubbed
  3   T. dried basil, crushed and rubbed
      salt
      pepper
  2   cloves garlic, minced
  1   large onion, finely chopped
  3   stalks celery, finely chopped
  1   medium bell pepper, finely chopped

Combine all of the ingredients in a large plastic bag, and marinate the catfish in it for 2-4 hours. Remove the catfish from the marinade and fill its cavity with the vegetables from the marinade. Place the catfish over a bed of hot coals in a smoker. Add 2 cups of water or more lemon-lime soda to the remaining marinade and fill the smoker pan. Smoke the catfish for 45 minutes. Remove fish from the smoker and place in a 350° oven for 20 minutes.

Serve with angel hair pasta or wild rice.

Blake A. Green
Dotham, Alabama

DEEP-FRIED CATFISH

	catfish fillets	2	cups corn meal
	water	1	cup flour
	salt	1	T. Creole seasoning
	buttermilk		peanut oil

Place fish in glass dish; add water to cover mixed with salt. Let stand about 10 minutes. Drain off the water and put enough buttermilk in to cover the fish. Let stand 30 minutes. Combine cornmeal, flour and seasoning in a plastic or brown paper bag. Drain fillets and shake them in the bag a few at a time.

In a deep frying pan or Dutch oven, heat the peanut oil on high heat. Add the fish to the oil when the oil is hot. Cook until the fish are golden brown. Place fish on paper towels to drain. Can be kept warm in the oven while other dishes are cooking.

Otis McNeal
Mt. Vernon, Georgia

WESTERN STYLE CATFISH ON THE GRILL

1 whole catfish, gutted, with the head removed
   (6-8 lbs.)
   salt
   pepper
3 medium onions, quartered
1 cup barbecue sauce
6 slices bacon
   fresh lemon
   melted butter with garlic

Place the fish on a large piece of double layered foil. Salt and pepper the cavity then stuff with onions and barbecue sauce. Place 3 strips of bacon on each side of the fish skin. Wrap fish tightly in the foil. Place the foil package on a hot grill for 10-15 minutes per side.

Serve with fresh lemon, and melted butter with a touch of garlic.

Rod Mach
Omaha, Nebraska

CATFISH' N HUSH PUPPY REVERIE

For Fish:

2½ lbs. catfish fillets
     buttermilk, milk, or beer (for a marinade)
1½ cups yellow cornmeal
½ cup all-purpose flour
1 T. salt (optional)
2 T. garlic powder
1 tsp. onion powder
1 tsp. paprika
2 T. crushed red pepper flakes
1 tsp. Creole or Cajun seasoning (optional)
1 egg
     oil for frying

For Hush Puppies:

6 green onions
1 egg
1 tsp. baking powder
     yellow cornmeal

To prepare fish: Trim all bloodlines from fish, rinse and place in a plastic container; completely cover with buttermilk, milk or beer and refrigerate. After desired marinating time, drain the fish, reserving the marinade. Mix all dry ingredients; add 1 egg and enough marinade until batter is of pancake batter consistency. Preheat oil in skillet to 375°. Dip fish in batter and fry approximately 2-3 minutes per side, until golden brown. Drain on paper towels.

To make hush puppies: Dice the green onions and add to any remaining fish batter. Add 1 egg and baking powder, and gradually stir in cornmeal until you have a cake-batter consistency. Add a heaping tablespoon of batter to same oil used for fish and fry over medium heat until golden brown. Drain on paper towels.

Serve immediately with french fries, lemon wedges, a bottle of your favorite hot sauce, and ice tea or a frosted mug of your favorite lager.

Dan Morris Sr.
Science Hill, Kentucky

CHANNEL CAT STEW

- 2 lbs. catfish fillets, chopped
- 2½ T. flour
- 2½ T. olive oil
- 1 medium onion, chopped
- 3 cloves garlic, minced
- 1 bell pepper, chopped
- 1 rib of celery, chopped
- 7 cups water
- 2 medium potatoes, chopped
- 1 tsp. paprika
- ¼ tsp. cayenne
- ¼ tsp. dried thyme
- 1 bay leaf
- 6 green onions, chopped
  croutons

Heat the oil in a large soup pot. Mix in the flour, onion, garlic, bell pepper, and celery; cook, stirring until the vegetables are soft. Add the water, fish, potatoes and spices; cook on medium heat for 20-30 minutes, or until the potatoes are soft. Serve with green onions and croutons.

Terry J. McKibbin
Lawrenceville, Illinois

FRIED CATFISH WITH JALAPEÑO TARTAR SAUCE

    2   lbs. catfish fillets (1" thick)
    1   cup yellow cornmeal
        salt
        pepper
    2   tsp. garlic powder
    2   tsp. paprika
  ¼   cup milk
        vegetable oil
        lemon wedges

In a mixing bowl, combine the cornmeal, salt, pepper, garlic powder and paprika. Dip the fillets in the milk and dredge in the cornmeal mixture; set aside. Pour vegetable oil into a cast-iron skillet to a depth of ¼ inch, and heat over medium heat. Fry the fish 2-3 minutes per side, or until golden brown. Drain, and serve with jalapeño tartar sauce (recipe below) and lemon wedges.

Jalapeño Tartar Sauce:

    1   cup mayonnaise or whipped salad dressing
    2   T. finely chopped onions
    1   clove garlic, minced
  ¼   cup sweet-pepper relish
    1   T. lemon juice
    2   jalapeño peppers, seeded and minced

Combine all ingredients in a bowl and chill.

Carl Gerace
La Habra, California

TIDWELL'S SOUTHERN FRIED CATFISH FILLETS

2-3 lbs. catfish fillets	1 tsp. garlic powder
2 cups yellow cornmeal	2 cups cooking oil
3/4 cup flour	1 large onion
1 T. salt	2 large lemons
1 T. pepper	

Combine cornmeal, flour, salt, pepper and garlic powder in large paper sack. Shake to mix. Add fish fillets to sack and shake well. In a large pan or cast-iron skillet, heat the oil until a pinch of flour mixture fries. Add the fish fillets; cook slowly, turning fillets occasionally until golden brown.

Cut onion and lemons into wedges to garnish catfish fillets on the serving platter.

Richard Tidwell
Clanton, Alabama

LARRY'S DEEP FRIED CATFISH

1 lb. catfish fillets
1/2 cup flour
1/2 cup yellow cornmeal
1/2 tsp. salt
1/8 tsp. pepper
1/2 cup milk
4 cups corn oil

Mix the dry ingredients in a bowl. Dip the fillets in milk and then dredge in the flour mixture. Pour the corn oil into a heavy 3-quart saucepan, filling it no more than 1/3 full. Heat the oil to 375°. Fry the fish for 1½ minutes on each side. Drain on a paper towel and serve with hush puppies and coleslaw.

Larry Penn
Centre, Alabama

CODFISH SALAD

1	box salted codfish (or make your own homemade)	1	jar green olives
		1	medium onion, diced
		6	hard-boiled eggs, sliced
1	can chickpeas (garbanzo beans), rinsed and drained	6	large potatoes, peeled cut in bite-size pieces
			olive oil
1	can black olives		vinegar

Soak the codfish in water overnight. Cook the fish in boiling water until it flakes with a fork; then cool. Boil the potatoes; then cool. Combine all the ingredients, except oil and vinegar, in a bowl; use the olive oil and vinegar as a dressing.

Jana DaSilva
Glover, Vermont

BILL'S BAKED COD

2	lbs. skinned cod fillets	1	T. Worcestershire
1/4	cup mayonnaise		cayenne or hot pepper sauce
1/2	cup dry bread crumbs		salt
1/2	cup. butter		pepper
	juice of 1/2 a lemon		
	juice of 1/2 a lime	2	strips bacon

Cut the fish fillets into 4-6 ounce portions and place them on a buttered cookie sheet. With a pastry brush, coat each fillet with mayonnaise. Top each fillet with an even coat of bread crumbs. Melt the butter and add the lemon and lime juices, Worcestershire sauce, cayenne and hot pepper sauce. Sprinkle the butter sauce evenly over the fillets and season with salt and pepper to taste. Place a 2 inch strip of bacon on top of each filet. Bake in a 350° oven for 20-30 minutes, or until the fish and the bacon are done.

For a variation: Crushed cornflakes can be substituted for bread crumbs.

William L. Sisk
Cortez, Florida

MUSTARD CRAPPIE

10-12 crappie fillets
     mustard
  1 T. your favorite herb seasoning
  1 tsp. garlic salt
  1 cup seasoned bread crumbs
     oil for frying

Cut the fillets into bite-size pieces. Wash the fish, and while still very wet, put them in enough mustard to cover them. Let them marinate for 1 hour. Mix the dry ingredients in a paper bag. Remove the fish from the mustard marinade and shake in the bag until they are coated with the dry ingredients. Fry in hot oil in a deep-fryer until the pieces float to the top and are golden brown.

Clarke M. Williams III
Hayward, Wisconsin

"POOR MAN'S" CRAPPIE

12-15 crappie fillets
  1/4 cup butter or margarine
  1 T. garlic salt
  2 T. seasoning salt
  1 pinch black pepper
  1 pinch parsley

Dab the bottom of a 9 inch square non-stick pan with butter or margarine. Place the crappie fillets on top of the butter and sprinkle evenly with all of the seasonings. Cover the pan with aluminum foil and poke some holes in the foil so the steam will escape. Cook in a 400° oven for 5-7 minutes, or until the fish becomes flaky and white.

Lenny Gale
Nashua, New Hampshire

CRAPPIE COCKTAIL

1½ lbs. crappie fillets
1 16-oz. bottle Italian dressing
1 16-oz. bottle cocktail sauce
1 box toothpicks

Cut the crappies into several thin strips, approximately ¾ inch wide. Marinate them in the refrigerator in the Italian dressing for 2-3 hours. Roll the strips up and secure each roll with a toothpick.

Bring a large kettle of water to a furious boil. Place all the strips into the boiling water for 12-14 minutes. Carefully remove the pieces and drain well.

Place all of the toothpicked strips into a bowl, or arrange them nicely on a platter, and refrigerate them for 45 minutes to 1 hour.

Serve crappies with cocktail sauce or whatever sauce suits your fancy.

Kevin Grant
Colorado Springs, Colorado

MICROWAVE CRAPPIE

8 crappie fillets
1 cup pork flavored shakable baking mix
1 cup chicken flavored shakable baking mix
½ lemon
salt
pepper

Salt and pepper fillets to taste and squeeze a small amount of lemon juice on each slab. Mix pork and chicken shaking mixes together and place in a pie plate. Roll fillets in mixture and microwave in microwave safe dish on high for 4 minutes. Turn crappie over, and microwave for 4 more minutes or until fillets are flaky.

William R. Baker
Deltona, Florida

MIDWEST CRAPPIE

- 2 lbs. crappie fillets
- 2 eggs
- ½ cup milk
- 1 cup pancake mix
  salt
  pepper
  oil for frying

Beat eggs and mix well with milk. In a separate bowl, combine pancake mix and salt and pepper to taste. Dip fillets in egg and milk mixture, then coat with the pancake mixture. Drop fillets into a deep-fryer and cook until golden brown.

William R. Baker
Deltona, Florida

PANCAKE CRAPPIE

- 2 lbs. crappie fillets
- 1 egg, slightly beaten
- 2 T. teriyaki sauce
- 2 T. milk
- 1½ cups pancake mix
- 1 tsp. garlic salt
- 1 tsp. onion salt
  pepper
  vegetable oil

In a bowl, mix together egg, teriyaki sauce and milk. In a separate bowl, combine pancake mix, garlic salt, onion salt and pepper. Dip fillets first in egg mixture, then in pancake mixture. In a skillet, fry fillets in vegetable oil until golden brown.

Dale R. Britt
Canyon Lake, California

GRILLED CRAPPIE

16 crappie fillets
    non-stick vegetable spray
    dried oregano
    paprika
1-2 onions, sliced
1-2 tomatoes, sliced
  1 green pepper, sliced (optional)
    butter

Marinade:

½ cup vegetable oil
½ cup white or cider vinegar
 1 egg
 1 tsp. salt
 1 T. poultry seasoning
 1 tsp. pepper

Beat the marinade ingredients together in a large bowl. Add the fish and marinate for 30 minutes, stirring once or twice.

Fold up the edges of a heavy-duty sheet of aluminum foil about ¾ inch, to make a tray for grilling. Spray the foil with the cooking spray. Place the fish on the foil, sprinkle with the oregano and the paprika. Place the tomatoes and onions on top of the fish. (If you like green peppers, place them on top, as well.)

Grill, with the lid closed, for about 30 minutes over medium-high heat or until the fish is barely done; don't overcook. Add butter while cooking, if needed for moisture and to prevent sticking.

Robert N. Cassetty
Hendersonville, Tennessee

POPCORN CRAWFISH

1   lb. crawfish tails, shelled
    salt
    pepper
2   eggs, beaten
1/2 cup milk
    flour seasoned with salt, cayenne and
     garlic powder

Season crawfish with salt and pepper to taste. Dip in a mixture of eggs and milk, then dip in the flour. Fry crawfish in hot oil quickly.

Daryl Hoffmann
Harvey, North Dakota

CRAWFISH JAMBALAYA -OR-
IF YOU CAN'T CATCH A FISH, EAT YOUR BAIT!

1   lb. shelled cooked crawfish tails (2$1/2$ cups)
2   T. butter
1   cup chopped green pepper
1   cup sliced celery
1   cup sliced green onions
1   cup uncooked white rice
1   small can diced tomatoes
1   tsp. salt
1   tsp. poultry seasoning
1   clove garlic, minced
1/8-1/2 tsp. cayenne
1$1/2$ cups chicken broth

Heat the butter in a large skillet over medium-high heat. Add the green pepper, celery and green onions. Sauté until tender. Stir in the rest of the ingredients, except the crawfish. Bring to a boil, reduce the heat, cover and simmer for 25-30 minutes, or until the rice is tender. Stir in crawfish and cook until crawfish is hot.

Daryl Hoffmann
Harvey, North Dakota

Darryl Conrad

CRACKER FISH

2-2¹/₂ lbs. dolphin fillets,
    1¹/₂ " thick
1   cup mayonnaise
¹/₂   cup yellow mustard
3   cups crushed crackers

Mix the mayonnaise and mustard together. Coat the fish well on both sides with the mixture and then roll in the cracker crumbs. Place the fish in a greased glass baking dish and cover with any remaining crumbs. Cover the dish, and bake at 325° for 35 minutes Uncover for the last few minutes to brown the crumbs, if desired.

This recipe also works with boneless chicken breasts and leftovers make great sandwiches.

Darryl Conrad
Ft. Meyers, Florida

PRESSURE COOKER DRUM

1 drum fish, cleaned
1 can stewed tomatoes
1 small onion, chopped
2 garlic cloves, chopped
   salt
   pepper

Cut fish into pieces that will fit in your pressure cooker. Add remaining ingredients. Cook at 10 pounds pressure for 10 minutes.

Emery E. Neff, Jr.
Hermitage, Missouri

DEEP FRIED EEL POUT HORS D'OEUVRES IN BEER BATTER

   eel pout, or your favorite fish
1 can beer
2 cups flour
1 tsp. lemon pepper
   salt to taste
   oil for frying
   tartar sauce or seafood sauce

Skin and debone eel pout. Wash the meat thoroughly and cut into bite-size pieces. To make the batter, pour the beer into a glass and let stand for several hours until it is flat. Mix the flour, lemon pepper and salt together. Slowly pour beer into flour mixture until it turns paste-like. Coat the fish pieces completely with batter. Place the fish pieces in a deep-fryer. The pieces will sink at first. When they float up, cook an additional 4-5 minutes, until golden brown. Serve with toothpicks and bowls of tartar sauce and seafood sauce for dipping.

David Stokes
Duluth, Minnesota

FLOUNDER ROLL-UPS NORDAISE

2	cups sliced mushrooms (morels, in season)
	salt and pepper
5	T. butter, divided
2	egg yolks, slightly beaten
3/4	cup cream
1	cup grated cheddar cheese
1	cup cooked rice
10	flounder fillets (bass or crappie can be used)
	lemon juice
	thyme or parsley sprigs

Sauté the mushrooms in 2 tablespoons of butter for 5 minutes. Salt and pepper to taste, and set aside.

To make the Nordaise sauce: Melt 3 tablespoons of butter in another saucepan. Mix the egg yolks and cream together. Add to pan with ½ cup grated cheese, salt and pepper. Stir over medium heat until sauce thickens. Stir in ½ of the sautéed mushrooms. Set aside

To make the filling: Combine the remaining sautéed mushrooms, ½ cup cheese and cooked rice in a bowl. Stir in ¼ cup of Nordaise sauce and mix well.

Lightly sprinkle salt and lemon juice on the flounder fillets. Place ⅓ cup of filling on each fillet, roll up fillet, and place seam-down in a baking dish. Pour the remaining Nordaise sauce over the roll-ups.

Bake in a 375° oven for 20-25 minutes, or until the fish flakes when touched with a fork. Remove the fish from the baking dish with a spatula and garnish with sprigs of thyme or parsley.

Jeffrey Fee
Lancaster, Ohio

MICROWAVE FLOUNDER FILLETS

flounder fillets
1 can cream of shrimp soup
1 can water or milk
2 T. butter

fresh broccoli
seasoning salt
shredded cheese of your choice

Mix the soup and the water or milk in a glass bowl. Add the butter and microwave on high for 4 minutes covered.

Microwave the fresh broccoli in a second bowl with a small amount of water for 4 minutes on high. Sprinkle with seasoning salt and then place the broccoli evenly on the flounder fillets and roll fish around broccoli; securing toothpicks. Place rolls in the shrimp soup, sprinkle with the shredded cheese, cover with plastic wrap, and microwave on high for 10 minutes.

Robert Glenn Burcham
Woodlawn, Virginia

STUFFED FISH FILLETS

12 flounder fillets
1 egg
1/4 cup milk
onion powder
garlic powder

salt
pepper
4 cups prepared stuffing
paprika

Mix the egg and the milk together and set aside. Season all fillets to taste with the onion powder, garlic poweder, salt and pepper. Lay 4 fillets flat on a cookie sheet. Put a scoop of stuffing in the center of each fillet. Wrap 2 fillets crosswise around the stuffing on each fillet. Brush everything with the egg mixture and sprinkle with paprika. Bake in a 350° oven for 30-45 minutes.

Serve with your favorite vegetable and russet potatoes.

Frank Marcano
Yonkers, New York

MUSHROOM-TOPPED FLOUNDER

1	lb. flounder fillets
1/2	cup chopped onion
1/2	cup chopped celery
1/4	cup butter or margarine
1	lb. fresh mushrooms, sliced
1/3	cup white wine
1/4	tsp. salt
1/8	tsp. pepper
1	lemon
3	T. grated parmesan cheese
	salt
	pepper

Preheat the oven to 450°. Spray a shallow baking pan with non-stick cooking spray and arrange the fish in the pan. In a small skillet, over medium heat, sauté the onion and celery in butter until tender. Add the mushrooms, wine, salt, and pepper. Stir until the mushrooms are soft. Spoon evenly over fish. Sprinkle with lemon juice. Bake 8-10 minutes, until the fish flakes easily with a fork.

Robert Pertowski
Brooklyn, New York

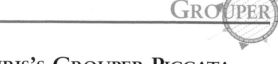

BRETT AND CHRIS'S GROUPER PICCATA

Brett and Chris Ridenour

	grouper fillets		juice of ½ a lemon
1	cup flour	2	T. capers
¼	cup butter		salt
1	cup white wine		pepper

In a large skillet, melt the butter over medium heat. Coat the fish with flour and add a dash of salt and pepper. Cook the fish for 10 minutes on each side, or until the fish flakes easily. Remove fish to a serving platter. Add white wine, lemon juice and capers to the skillet. Simmer until sauce is reduced, pour over the fish and serve.

Put a piece of fish on the top of your head and your tongue will beat your brains out trying to get at it.

Brett and Chris Ridenour
Palm Harbor, Florida

BAKED FISH EN PAPILLOTE

6   firm grouper fillets
    salt
    freshly ground black pepper
4   ripe plum tomatoes, seeded and slivered
1   red, yellow or orange bell pepper, cored,
      seeded, and slivered
1   T. capers, drained
2   T. chopped flat-leaf parsley
2   T. fresh lemon juice
2   T. extra-virgin olive oil

Cut 6 pieces of parchment paper (can substitute aluminum foil) to 14 x 12 inch size. Preheat the oven to 400°. Center on the lower half of each piece of parchment paper, and season with salt and pepper. Arrange the vegetables equally on top of each piece of fish and sprinkle with capers and parsley. Drizzle each fillet with 1 teaspoon lemon juice and 1 teaspoon olive oil.

Fold the top half of the parchment over the fish and crimp the edges on all sides to seal the packets. Place the packets on a baking sheet, leaving 2 inches between each one for proper heat circulation. Bake for 20 minutes. Let rest for 5 minutes before serving.

Eugene Cord
Chattanooga, Tennessee

LEMONY STUFFED HADDOCK FILLETS

2 lbs. fresh or frozen haddock fillets
2 T. butter or margarine
1 chopped green onion
1/4 cup chopped green pepper
1/4 cup celery
2 cups fresh bread cubes
1 tsp. grated lemon peel
1 T. lemon juice
  dash of salt
  dash of pepper
1 tsp. dry parsley flakes
1 T. melted butter
  snipped chives
  parsley sprigs
  lemon slices

Arrange half of the fillets in a greased casserole dish. Sauté the onion, green pepper and celery in butter until tender. Stir in the next 6 ingredients and toss well. Spoon the stuffing over the fillets, top with remaining fillets and brush with melted butter. Sprinkle with chives. Cover and bake at 450°, allowing 10 minutes per 1 inch of thickness. Uncover during the last 5-7 minutes. Garnish with parsley and lemon slices.

Leo G. J. Seffelaar
Broadview, Saskatchewan

Ronald Johnston

FISH 'N' CHIPS

	halibut fillets	½	tsp. paprika
1	cup flour	1	egg
¼	tsp. baking powder	1	Tbsp. melted butter
1½	tsp. salt	½	cup or more of milk
1½	tsp. pepper		

Mix the dry ingredients, then add enough egg, butter and milk to make a batter. Cut the halibut fillets into ¾ x 2 inch strips. Put the fish in the batter and stir. Deep fry the fish in hot oil (365°-375°) until golden brown. Enjoy with your favorite french fries.

Ronald Johnston
Sacramento, California

HALIBUT OLYMPIAN

2-4 halibut fillets
1 medium onion, diced
1 T. clarified butter
  salt
  pepper
6 T. mayonnaise
1 T. Dijon mustard
1 T. fresh lemon juice
  fresh dill weed to garnish
  diced tomatoes to garnish

Debone and then trim any fat and skin from the fillets. Sauté the onion in butter until translucent. Season with salt and pepper. In a medium casserole or cake pan, spread the onions evenly over the bottom. Take the cleaned halibut fillets, pat them dry and lay them over the onions.

Whisk together the mayonnaise, mustard, lemon juice, and a pinch of salt and pepper. Smear the halibut fillets with this sauce. Cover the casserole with a lid or foil, and bake in a 300° oven for 15 minutes, or until the meat flakes. Turn the oven up to 475° and bake for 6-8 minutes or until fillets are golden. Garnish with fresh dill weed and diced tomatoes.

Goes great with broccoli spears fresh from the garden.

Rob McQuinn
Independence, Missouri

HALIBUT VERA CRUZ

       1   halibut steak
           flour
           clarified butter
      1/4 avocado, sliced
       1   piece of green chili, sliced
       4   black olives, sliced
      1/2 tomato, diced
       2   green onions, chopped
           salt
           pepper
       1   tsp. Cajun spice*
     1 1/2 T. tequila
           juice of a large wedge of lemon
           shredded Monterey Jack cheese

Lightly flour the halibut and then sauté in clarified butter, adding the rest of the ingredients, except the cheese. (Note: Never add alcohol over an open flame. Move the skillet away from the stove and wait 1 minute after adding the alcohol before returning it to the stove.)

When fish is cooked, place it on a plate and cover with the mixture in the skillet and the shredded cheese.

*Cajun Spice
      1/2 cup paprika
      1/4 cup salt
      1/4 cup onion powder
      1/4 cup garlic powder
      1/4 cup cayenne
      1/4 cup black pepper
       2   T. dried thyme leaves
       2   T. dried oregano leaves

Harold Eurich
Colfax, California

CHEESY HALIBUT BAKE

Doug Oppelt

2   lbs. halibut fillets
    seasoned salt
½   medium onion,
    chopped
2   cups shredded
    medium Cheddar
    cheese,
1   cup mayonnaise
½   cup Parmesan
    cheese
2   T. chopped fresh
    parsley
I   T. paprika

Preheat oven to 350°. Cut halibut into 3 inch cubes and lay them evenly in a glass baking dish. Sprinkle halibut with seasoned salt.

In a bowl, mix onion, cheese and mayonnaise. Spread this mixture evenly over the halibut, then sprinkle with the parmesan, parsley and paprika. Cover and bake for 30 minutes.

Doug Oppelt
Milton, Washington

BAKED HALIBUT

halibut steaks
mayonnaise
baby bay shrimp, deveined and peeled, cooked or
   frozen
crab meat, cooked or frozen, shredded

Preheat the oven to 350°. Line a 9 x 13-glass dish with aluminum foil. Spread mayonnaise on both sides of the halibut and place fish on the foil. Sprinkle to taste with the baby bay shrimp. Sprinkle the shredded crab meat over the halibut and shrimp. Cover with foil and bake for about 1 hour. If a crisper surface is desired, remove the foil for the last 5-10 minutes.

Good reheated or cold.

William E. Hux
Bullhead City, Arizona

SMOKED MULLET

4-6 fresh mullet
1-2 cups hickory or oak wood chips
¼ cup salt
1 cup butter
¼ cup lemon juice
¼ cup Worcestershire sauce

One day ahead: Soak the wood chips in water. Dress fish, leaving the scales on. Split the fish in half leaving the 2 halves together at the back. Put the fish in a dish of water to cover and stir in the salt. Refrigerate overnight.

Cooking time: Use an outdoor grill and get the coals very hot. Spread the wood chips over the top of the hot coals. Cover the rack on the grill with aluminum foil. In a pan melt the butter; add lemon juice, and Worcestershire sauce. Use this mixture to baste the fish while it is cooking. Fish is done when bones come out easily and fish flakes with fork.

Otis McNeal
Mt. Vernon, Georgia

POACHED PANFISH

8   oz. panfish fillets
1   T. butter
¼   cup white cooking
    wine
    pinch of thyme
    pinch of rosemary
    pinch of basil
1   tsp. lemon juice

Melt the butter in a frying pan and add the wine, the herbs and the lemon juice; bring to a slow boil. Lay the fillets in the pan and turn immediately to coat both sides evenly. Cover. The cooking time depends on the thickness of the fillets. When you can easily flake the fillets with a fork, they are done. It usually takes no more than 5 minutes.

Serve with rice. This dish makes a good alternative to deep-fried fish that has too much crust.

Greg Stetz
Pelican Rapids, Minnesota

Greg Stetz-- Nice try, Greg!!!

"This dish makes a good alternative to deep fried fish that has too much crust."

CREAMY POACHED PANFISH

1½ lbs. panfish fillets
½ cup sliced fresh mushrooms
2 T. cooking oil
1 cup dry white wine
2 T. butter
¼ cup heavy cream
  salt
  pepper
  paprika
  parsley sprigs

In a small frying pan, sauté the mushrooms in oil for 5 minutes. Set aside. Put the wine and the butter in a large frying pan and bring to a boil. Add the fillets and return to a boil. Reduce the heat and simmer for 5 minutes, or until the fillets flake when probed with a fork. Remove fillets from pan and place on a heated platter in a 150° oven.

Over high heat, reduce the poaching liquid to ¼ cup. Add the cream and the mushrooms. Bring the sauce to a boil, stirring constantly. Add salt and pepper to taste, and spoon over the fillets. Dust the fillets with paprika and garnish with parsley sprigs.

Norma Blank
Shawano, Wisconsin

ZESTY PANFISH FILLETS

8-10 panfish fillets
1 cup flour*
1/8 tsp. salt
1/8 tsp. pepper
6-8 oz. zesty Italian salad dressing*
oil for frying

Marinate the fish fillets in Italian dressing in a shallow pan for 1/2 hour. Coat the fillets in a flour, salt, and pepper mixture. Pan fry in a hot oiled frying pan until golden brown on both sides.

*Flour and dressing amounts will vary based on size of fillets used.

Rodney D. Schultz
Beloit, Wisconsin

STEAMED WHOLE FISH

2-3 lbs. whole perch or graysole, cleaned and scaled
1 T. fresh ginger, sliced thin
3 green onions, sliced into thin strips
1 tsp. sugar
1/2 T. soy sauce
1/4 cup peanut or corn oil
fresh cilantro sprigs
pepper

Make 3 diagonal slashes on each side. Place fish on a steaming platter and steam for 8-10 minutes, or until cooked. Discard remaining steaming water, sprinkle fish with sugar, and place the green onions and ginger on the fish. Heat the cooking oil in a small saucepan until hot but not smoking, then pour it on the fish. It will sizzle. Pour on the soy sauce, sprinkle with pepper, and garnish with cilantro. Serve.

Neng-Yi Yao
Rowland Heights, California

BROWN-CRISPY-FRIED PANFISH

18 panfish fillets
3 cups flour
1/2 tsp. salt
    pepper to taste
    shortening

Put flour, salt, and pepper in a mixing bowl, and coat fillets thoroughly with mixture. Melt shortening over medium heat. Fry fillets for about 15 minutes, or until brown and crispy.

William Bradley
Vienna, Ohio

DEEP-FRIED PANFISH

    panfish fillets
2 eggs
1/2 tsp. salt
1/2 tsp. pepper
1/4 cup milk
    bread crumbs
    shortening

Combine eggs, salt, pepper and milk in a bowl. Put the bread crumbs in a small pan. Melt shortening on high heat. Dip the fish in egg mixture, then in bread crumbs, coating thoroughly. Put the fillets into the hot shortening and cook about 5 minutes per side, until brown. Remove to paper-towel-lined tray and serve hot.

William Bradley
Vienna, Ohio

John Harris

PERCH BOOYAH

2	dozen perch fillets	2	T. pepper
5	ribs of celery, finely chopped	1	dozen medium potatoes, cubed small
2	onions, chopped	1	lb. butter
4	T. salt	2	large cans tomato soup

Fill a 10-quart pot ⅓ full of cold water. Add the perch and bring to a boil. Turn the heat down and simmer for 2 minutes. Remove the perch and save the water. Add the celery and the onions to the perch water. Cook on medium heat until tender. Add salt, pepper, potato cubes, tomato soup and 2 soup cans of water. Turn the heat down to simmer; add 2 sticks of butter at a time until melted. While simmering, add the perch, but break up the fillets and check for "Y" bones. Taste test and add salt or pepper, if desired. Turn off the stove and let soup sit for a few minutes. Can be frozen for eating another day.

John Harris
New Bloomfield, Missouri

LEMON PEPPER FRIED PERCH

    4   perch fillets
    1   cup all-purpse flour
    2   tsp. grated lemon peel
  1/2   tsp. salt
  1/2   tsp. pepper
    1   cup water
        vegetable oil
        flour for coating

Combine 1 cup flour, the lemon peel, salt and pepper in medium bowl. Stir in the water and cover. Place covered mixture in your refrigerator for at least 30 minutes.

In a deep frying pan heat 1½-3 inches of oil to 375°. Coat fish with additional flour, then dip in chilled batter. Fry a few pieces at a time, turning occasionally until light golden brown. Drain on paper towels. Repeat with remaining fish. Keep fried fish in a warm oven.

George Becker
Syracuse, New York

BEER-BATTER DEEP-FRIED PERCH

2½-3 lbs. perch fillets
1½ cups buttermilk
      pancake mix
  1   egg
1/2   tsp. black pepper
1/2   tsp. ground ginger

  1   tsp. salt
1/4   tsp. white pepper
1/2   tsp. dried thyme
1½   cups beer
      cooking oil, heated to 375°

Mix all ingredients, except the perch and the oil. Season the fillets with more salt and pepper, and cut into strips the size of your little finger. Dip the fillets in batter and let excess drip off. Put the fillets, one at a time, into the oil and fry until golden brown. Do not overcook. Drain on paper towels before serving.

Kevin Jurgovan
Posen, Illinois

CLAMS CASINO WITH PERCH

1 6-oz. can minced clams
½ lb. perch fillets
1 T. finely chopped onion
1 T. finely chopped red or green pepper
1 T. butter or margarine
1 T. Parmesan cheese
½ cup Italian bread crumbs
15-20 clam shell halves
dash of Worcestershire sauce or teriyaki sauce
dash bottled hot pepper sauce
3-4 strips of bacon
paprika
chopped parsley

Simmer the perch fillets in the clam juice from the canned clams for 2-3 minutes. Remove the perch, break into pieces and set aside; save the clam juice. Mix all of the other ingredients, except the clam shell halves, bacon, paprika and parsley, in a bowl; add the perch fillets and the clam juice.

Fry the bacon until well-done, cut into small pieces or crumble, and set aside. Spoon the perch mixture into clam shells and sprinkle with paprika and chopped parsley. Put the bacon bits on top; add a dab of butter for moisture if desired. Place the clam shells on a baking sheet and bake at 450° for 7 minutes.

If there are any leftovers they can be wrapped and frozen for later use. And yes, the shells can be recycled.

Rodger D. McKeon
Rochester, New York

CITRUS BATTER-FRIED FISH

perch fillets
1   cup flour
1/2 cup yellow cornmeal
1   tsp. salt
1   tsp. pepper
grated rind from 1 lemon or orange
beaten eggs or canned milk
oil or shortening for frying

Shake the flour, cornmeal, salt, pepper, and lemon or orange rind in a paper or plastic bag until well mixed. Dry the fish, dip them in the beaten eggs or canned milk, and then shake them in the bag with the dry mixture until they are well coated. Fry the fish in hot oil or shortening until done, approximately 3-4 minutes per side.

Enjoy the fish with cold beans and fried potatoes.

John Sikorski
Williamsville, New York

PERCH SALSA

8 perch, filleted
4 tomatoes, chopped
2 green peppers, chopped
2 white onions, minced
1 jalapeño pepper, minced
½ cup olive oil
¼ cup red wine vinegar
¼ cup lime juice
1 T. chopped fresh cilantro
   dash of salt
   dash of black pepper

Preheat oven to 350°. Arrange the perch in a baking pan. Mix all other ingredients and pour over the perch. Bake for 15 minutes, or until fish is done.

Brad Sime
Merrillville, Indiana

ITALIAN MARINATED BARBECUED PIKE

  4 pike steaks
 1/2 cup olive oil
 1/4 cup white wine vinegar
  3 cloves garlic, minced
  1 T. chopped fresh oregano
  1 T. chopped fresh basil
  1 T. chopped fresh parsley
     juice from 1 whole lemon
 1/2 T. fresh cracked pepper
  1 whole lemon, cut into 8 wedges
  4 sprigs fresh oregano

Combine the olive oil, vinegar, garlic, oregano, basil, parsley, lemon juice and pepper to form a marinade for the steaks. Marinate the steaks for 30-45 minutes, turning them several times. Remove steaks from marinade and place the steaks on heavy-duty foil on a plate, reserving the marinade to baste the steaks. Have the grill preheated to a moderate heat. Place a metal pan, which will act as a drip pan on the coals. Place the cooking grid 4 inches above the coals.

Slide the steaks off the plate, foil-side-down, onto the grill over the drip pan. Baste the fish often during the cooking time. Turn the steaks only once and keep the grill covered during the cooking process. When the fish is cooked, remove with a spatula to plates and garnish with the lemon wedges and the oregano sprigs. Discard any remaining marinade.

Note: Cook the fish for 8-10 minutes for each inch of fish. Pike is flaky and becomes dry if overcooked.

Richard Mullvain
Duluth, Minnesota

PIKE A LA LICHON

2 boneless pike fillets
3 T. olive oil
1 medium onion, sliced
1 green bell pepper, sliced
1 rib celery, chopped
2 cloves garlic, chopped
1 tsp. margarine or butter
1 T. grated Parmesan
    cheese

Heat olive oil in a large skillet. Add onion, pepper, celery and garlic sauté for 5 minutes. Remove pan from heat and set aside.

Line a shallow baking pan with foil. Place the fillets in the pan and cover with the vegetables and olive oil from the skillet. Put ½ teaspoon of margarine or butter on each filet.

Broil the fish for approximately 10 minutes, or until the meat is an opaque white. Just before the fish is done cooking, add the Parmesan cheese and finish cooking.

Paul Lichon
Saginaw, Michigan

Paul Lichon

FISH PINWHEELS

4 northern pike or other lean fish fillets, ¼ inch thick, 12-15 inches long	½ cup herb-seasoned stuffing mix
½ cup chopped fresh mushrooms	2 T. hot water
2 T. chopped celery	½ tsp. salt
2 T. chopped onion	⅛ tsp. pepper
3 T. margarine, divided	⅛ tsp. ground sage
	1½ cups mushroom sauce*

Heat the oven to 375°. Grease an 8 x 4 inch loaf pan. In a small skillet, cook mushrooms, celery and onion in 2 tablespoons of margarine over medium heat until tender. Remove the skillet from the heat. Add the herb-seasoned stuffing mix, hot water, salt, pepper and sage to the vegetables. Stir until the mixture is moistened. Spread ¼ of the stuffing mixture evenly on each fillet, pressing lightly. Roll up the fillets, starting with the narrow ends. Place the rolls upright in the prepared pan, arranging in a staggered pattern. Brush with 1 tablespoon of melted margarine. Cover the pan with foil and bake until the fish in the center of each roll flakes easily, 30-35 minutes. Serve with warm mushroom sauce.

*Mushroom Sauce

2 cups chopped fresh mushrooms	¼ tsp. salt
¼ cup chopped onion	⅛ tsp. pepper
2 T. margarine or butter	⅓ cup milk
	¼ cup sour cream
1 T. flour	1 T. Dijon mustard
	1 T. white wine (optional)

In a small saucepan or skillet, cook and stir the mushrooms and onion in margarine over medium heat, until the onion is tender, about 5 minutes. Stir in flour, salt and pepper. Blend in the milk. Stir constantly until thickened, about 3 minutes. Remove from heat; stir in the sour cream, mustard and wine. Serve over the fish.

Makes 1½ cups sauce.

David Patrick Valverde
Seary, Arizona

PICKLED PIKE

   pike, cut into bite-size pieces
2 cups water
1 cup vinegar
1 cup brown sugar
1 onion, sliced
   coarse salt
   whole allspice

Combine water, vinegar and brown sugar in saucepan; bring to a boil, stirring until sugar is dissolved. Sprinkle the coarse salt on fish pieces. Place the fish into jars; add the allspice, onion, and brine. Refrigerate 2-3 weeks, depending on thickness of the fish. Recipe makes 2 quarts.

Steven Wallner
Mars, Pennsylania

NORTHERN PIKE AND CREAM CHEESE PÊTÉ

      leftover cooked pike
1   8-oz. container soft cream cheese
      chopped chives to taste
      finely chopped onion to taste
2   tsp. lemon juice
1/4   cup finely chopped red bell pepper
1/2   tsp. dried dill weed

Loosely chop the pike and mix with the other ingredients. Refrigerate for 1-2 hours to blend the flavors. Serve with your favorite crackers.

Harry O. Jacob
Saginaw, Michigan

KEN'S PICKLED FISH

fish fillets (northern pike works well), cut into
  bite-size pieces
salt water
white vinegar
sliced onions

For brine:
1   cup white port wine
2   cups white vinegar
1   cup sugar
2   T. pickling spices

Soak the fish fillets in salt water for 24 hours and then drain. Soak them in white vinegar for 24 hours and then drain. Prepare the brine by boiling the brine ingredients together. Allow the brine to cool. Layer the sliced onions and fish in glass canning jars, cover with the brine and tighten the lids. Refrigerate for 10 days; eat, and enjoy.

Great to take along to your hunting shack.

John H. Van Horn
Huntley, Illinois

POOR MAN'S LOBSTER

northern pike
1   small potato, coarsely chopped
1   onion, coarsely chopped
1   carrot, coarsely chopped
melted butter

Cut fish into 2-3 inch pieces. Boil potato, onion and carrot in water. Using a deep-fat fryer basket, lower the fish into the boiling water and cook for 7 minutes. Serve with the melted butter. If you want the fish to be a little brown, place under broiler before serving.

Bill Schoenberg
Hancock, Minnesota

Pickled Northern

Pike (the smaller northern pike works great)
1 cup pickling salt
3 cups water
1 cup white vinegar, plus enough to cover the
   fish with brine
1 cup sugar
1 T. mixed pickling spice
slice onions

Clean the fish and cut into bite-size pieces. There is no need to remove the bones. Skinning is optional. To make the brine, mix the salt in the water until dissolved. Place the fish in a crock and cover with brine. Refrigerate for 2 days, then pour off the brine and cover the fish with white vinegar for 24 hours. Drain. To make the syrup, combine 1 cup of white vinegar, sugar and pickling spice-boil for 5 minutes. Let cool. Layer the fish and the sliced onions in a jar and cover with syrup. Pike is ready to eat in a few days. And you won't find a bone.

Galen Brunner
Hartford, Wisconsin

BAKED FISH IN WHITE WINE

3-3½ lbs. pollock fillets
 ½ medium onion, sliced
 3 shallots, minced
 1 cup sliced mushrooms
 1 T. lemon juice
   salt
   pepper
   pinch ground nutmeg
   pinch ground cloves
   dry white wine
 2 T. brandy
 2 T. flour
 2 T. soft butter
   dash cayenne
   parsley (optional)
   lemon slices (optional)

Dry the fish. Butter a large baking dish and arrange the fish in it.
Separate the onions into rings. Scatter over the fish. Combine the
shallots, mushrooms, lemon juice, salt and pepper to taste, nutmeg
and cloves. Sprinkle over the fish. Add wine to almost cover the fish.

Bake at 350° for 20-30 minutes. Remove from the oven and drain all of
the cooking liquid to a small saucepan. Reduce the liquid over high heat
to 1¼ cups. Warm the brandy in a ladle and light carefully. Pour the
brandy into the reduced liquid. Set aside. Cream together the flour and
butter. Add to the liquid, stirring constantly, over medium heat. When
thick, add cayenne and pour over the fish. Garnish with parsley and
lemon slices.

Leo G. J. Seffelaar
Broadview, Saskatchewan

DAVE'S FISH CREOLE

1   lb. fish fillets, orange roughy or cod are great
1/4   cup flour
1/3   cup cooking oil
1   cup hot water
1   small can whole tomatoes
1/2   cup chopped green onions with tops
1/2   cup chopped parsley
1/4   cup chopped green pepper
4   small cloves garlic, finely chopped
1/2   tsp. salt
1/2   tsp. crushed dried thyme
1/4   tsp. cayenne pepper
2   whole bay leaves
1   slice lemon
2   cups cooked white rice

Thaw fish if frozen. Blend the flour into the hot oil and brown in large pot, stirring constantly. Add water gradually and cook until thick and smooth. Add all of the remaining ingredients, except rice. Cover and simmer for 20 minutes. Remove the bay leaves and serve over rice.

David Reid Cunnison
Denver, Colorado

"STILLED" ORANGE ROUGHY FILLETS

    2   6-oz. orange roughy fillets
  ½   cup water
  ½   cup dry white wine
    2   slices of lemon
    1   medium onion, sliced
    2   T. fresh herbs of your choice, chopped
    1   clove garlic, minced, or ½ tsp. chopped garlic in oil
  ¾   cup fresh sliced mushrooms

Place the fish fillets, water, wine, lemon, onion slices, herbs and garlic in a saucepan. Cover the pan and poach the fish over medium heat until tender, or until the fish flakes easily, 5-10 minutes. Remove the fish from the liquid and keep warm. Remove the lemon slices and discard. Add the sliced mushrooms to pan, return the pan to the heat and boil until the liquid is reduced by 1/4. Spoon the mushrooms and sauce over the fish and serve.

Leo G. J. Seffelaar
Broadview, Saskatchewan

MICROWAVE FISH FOR REALLY LAZY FISHERMEN

2   lbs. of salmon or trout fillets
4   T. butter
$\frac{1}{2}$ cup bread crumbs
3   T. minced finely
     chopped onion
$\frac{1}{4}$ tsp. poultry
     seasoning
    salt
    pepper

Melt the butter in a baking dish. Stir in half of the bread crumbs and the onion.

Microwave on high for two minutes. Combine the rest of the ingredients and coat the fillets. Place fillets in dish, turning to coat. Microwave on high for 6-7 minutes, turning once after 3 minutes.

Ron Jurgovan
Posen, Illinois

Ron Jurgovan

PERFECTION SALMON

1   fresh salmon
    lemon
    butter
    salt
    pepper

Place salmon on aluminum foil and add lemon, butter, salt and pepper to taste. Fold foil to create a water-tight seal around the fish. Place package in top rack of empty automatic dishwasher. Close the door and start the wash cycle. (Do not add the soap!) At the end of the cycle, remove the fish, unwrap and serve. Other seasonings can be added to create your own taste.

Jack Garrett
Wawaka, Indiana

SALMON WITH BROWN SUGAR-BUTTER SAUCE

2-4   salmon fillets or steaks
1/4   cup brown sugar
1/4   cup butter, melted
1-2   tsp. lemon juice
1-2   tsp. soy sauce

Melt the butter and mix with the sugar, lemon juice and soy sauce. Line a broiler pan with foil and place the salmon on the foil. Pour the mixture over the steaks. Broil until done.

Rod and Susanne Shafer
Salem, Oregon

COHO SALMON AND BEET SAUCE

2 lbs. coho salmon fillets
1 medium carrot, sliced
¼ cup sliced leeks
¼ cup sliced celery
1 T. diced fennel bulb
8 oz. beets, cooked and pureed
½ tsp. dried tarragon
½ tsp. dried summer savory
½ tsp. dried dill
   pinch ground cumin
2 T. heavy cream
   honey to sweeten
   lime juice
   salt
   pepper

Lightly sauté the carrot, leeks, celery and fennel. Add the beet purée and the spices, and lightly simmer for 15 minutes while gradually stirring in the cream. The sauce should have the texture of velvety applesauce. Finally, season to taste with honey, lime juice, salt and pepper. Grill or pan-fry the salmon and serve with the sauce.

Leo G. J. Seffelaar
Broadview, Saskatchewan

LIME-ZESTED SALMON

 4   4-oz. salmon fillets
 2   T. chopped green onions
 2   T. dry sherry
 1   T. fresh lime juice
1½   tsp. low-sodium soy sauce
 1   tsp. peeled, grated gingerroot
 1   tsp. vegetable oil
 ½   tsp. grated lime rind
 1   ripe mango, peeled and cut into 12 wedges

Place the salmon in an 8 inch square baking dish. Combine the green onions, sherry, lime juice, soy sauce, ginger, oil and lime rind. Pour over the salmon and marinate in the refrigerator for 30 minutes. Bake, uncovered, at 450° for 15 minutes, or until the salmon flakes easily when tested with a fork. Serve with the mango wedges.

This recipe goes great with seasoned wild rice and broiled tomato halves.

Leo G. J. Seffelaar
Broadview, Saskatchewan

SALMON WITH RADISH TARTAR

4   salmon steaks (6-8 oz. each)
1   lb. green beans
12 small red potatoes
4   butterhead lettuce leaves
1   lb. cherry tomatoes, stemmed

In a 6-quart pan, bring 3 quarts of water to a boil. Add the beans and cook until barely tender, about 5 minutes. Lift out and immerse in ice water until cool. Drain the beans and set aside. Return the water in the pan to a boil and add fish. Cover the pan tightly and remove from heat.

Let the fish stand just until opaque, but still moist in the thickest part (cut to test) about 12 minutes. Lift out and immerse in ice water until cool. Drain, pat dry and set aside. Return the water in the pan to a boil and add the potatoes, simmering until tender when pierced, 20-25 minutes. Drain the potatoes and immerse in ice water to cool. Drain and set aside.

Arrange the lettuce on a platter. Lay the salmon on top and arrange the beans, potatoes and tomatoes around the fish.

Serve with Radish Tartar.

Radish Tartar

1   cup plain low-fat yogurt
3/4   cup chopped red radishes
1/3   cup minced green onions
2   T. drained and rinsed capers
1   T. prepared horseradish

Combine all ingredients and chill.

Leo G. J. Seffelaar
Broadview, Saskatchewan

BAKED GINGER COHO SALMON

- 1 whole Coho salmon (3-4 lbs.)
- 1 tsp. ground ginger
- 1/2 tsp. ground allspice
  salt
  pepper
- 1 medium onion, sliced
- 2 carrots, thinly sliced
- 1 1/2 T. butter, cut into pats

Dry inside of fish. Rub salt, pepper, ginger and allspice into cavity. Insert onion and carrots into cavity. Place fish in an ungreased baking pan. Arrange butter pats on top of fish. Bake for 45 minutes at 350°

Ron Jurgovan
Posen, Illinois

Ron Jurgovan

SALMON BALL

1	large can salmon, drained and boned, or ½-pint jar of salmon
8	oz. cream cheese, softened
¼	tsp. liquid smoke
¼	cup finely chopped onion, or 2 T. grated onion
1	tsp. lemon juice
½	tsp. salt
	chopped nuts
	parsley

Mix all of the ingredients except for the chopped nuts and parsley. Roll into a ball, then roll in the chopped nuts and parsley. Refrigerate until ready to serve.

Freezes well.

Joseph J. Lifatich
Eugene, Oregon

EASY CANNED SALMON

salmon fillets
western salad dressing

Cut fish into 1½-2 inch pieces. Wash fish thoroughly. Pack pint canning jars half full with pieces. Add 1 tablespoon of salad dressing, fill jar with more salmon, then add another tablespoon of dressing. Place lids on jars and cook in a pressure cooker at 10 pounds for 100 minutes. Let the jars cool until sealed. Sealed jars will last a long time.

David Stokes
Duluth, Minnesota

BAKED SALMON

	salmon fillets
1	onion, chopped
½	cup Worcestershire sauce
¼	tsp. salt
¼	tsp. pepper
2	T. lemon juice

Place salmon in baking dish in single layer. Sprinkle onion, Worcestershire sauce, salt, pepper and lemon juice over salmon. Bake at 350° for 40 minutes.

Bruce Brulotte
Boardman, Oregon

VERMICELLI WITH SALMON AND FRESH VEGETABLES

2	cans salmon, drained and flaked (or you can use fresh)
1	T. butter
1	onion, finely chopped
3	cups milk
4	oz. cream cheese, cubed
1	T. chopped fresh dill, or 1 tsp. dried dill weed
1	carrot, cut into thin strips
	fresh vegetables of your choice, cut up
½	lb. uncooked vermicelli

In a saucepan, melt the butter over low heat. Add the onion and cook for 5 minutes, stirring occasionally. Stir in the milk, cheese and dill, cooking and stirring until the mixture is smooth and just reaches the boiling point. Add the vegetables and the salmon and simmer for 5 minutes. Cook the vermicelli according to the package directions. Toss the vermicelli with the salmon sauce. Garnish with a sprig of fresh dill.

Leo G. J. Seffelaar
Broadview, Saskatchewan

SALMON FILLETS WITH FENNEL SAUCE

4 salmon fillets with skin on
  salt
  pepper
1 bunch fennel leaves

Sauce:

2 T. butter
  juice of 2 lemons
2 T. chopped fresh fennel leaves
1/4 tsp. paprika
1 pinch of cayenne pepper
  salt
  pepper

Preheat the grill to medium heat. Salt and pepper the salmon and set aside. Arrange the fennel on the preheated cooking grid to form a bed for the salmon. Lay the fillets on top, skin side down. Cook, covered, without turning.

To make the sauce, melt butter in a heavy saucepan and whisk in all of the other sauce ingredients. Serve the fillets with a dollop of sauce.

Note: Because the salmon absorbs the delicate licorice flavor of the fennel when grilled on a bed of its leaves, the sauce can be omitted if desired.

Leo G. J. Seffelaar
Broadview, Saskatchewan

PAN-FRIED SALMON

5-6 lbs. salmon fillets
2 eggs
1/4 cup milk
1 tsp. black pepper
1 tsp. ground ginger
3/4 cup medium-fine yellow cornmeal
1/2 tsp. white pepper
1/2 tsp. dried thyme
2 tsp. garlic salt
3/4 cup flour
vegetable oil

Gently mix eggs and milk in a shallow pan. Mix all dry ingredients and spread out in a shallow pan. Cut the fillets into 4-6 ounce servings. Towel dry the cleaned fillets. Dip the fillets in the egg and milk mixture, then roll in the dry ingredients.

Put just enough oil in a large frying pan to keep the fish from sticking. Heat the oil until it begins to smoke, lay in the salmon fillets, and brown thoroughly on one side. Turn fillets over and brown the other side. Do not overcook. Drain on paper towels before serving.

Kevin Jurgovan

This mixture can be used for deep-frying, too.

Kevin Jurgovan
Posen, Illinois

SALMON CUTLETS

1	cup cooked salmon		1	tsp. grated onion
1½	cups mashed		1	egg
	potatoes		1	T. water
1	tsp. salt			bread crumbs
¼	tsp. pepper			oil for frying

Flake the salmon and add the potatoes, salt, pepper and onion to it, mixing well. Form the mixture into patties. Roll the patties first in the bread crumbs (seasoned or unseasoned, per individual taste), then dip in a slightly beaten egg and water combination, then again in the bread crumbs. Fry in a deep fryer for 3 minutes at 380°. Serve with salmon cutlet sauce. (recipe below)

Sauce for Salmon Cutlets

- 2 cups strained tomatoes
- 1 T. butter
- 1 T. sugar
- 2 bay leaves
- 1 T. flour
- salt
- pepper

Combine all ingredients in a saucepan and cook over medium heat for 5 minutes. Strain sauce and spoon sauce onto cutlets, then serve.

R. Marlinelli
Erie, Pennsylvania

GRILLED SALMON WITH DILL SAUCE

4	large salmon steaks	1	tsp. dry mustard
1/2	cup mayonnaise	1/4	tsp. garlic powder
1/4	cup sour cream	1/8	tsp. sugar
1 1/2	T. chopped fresh dill	1/8	tsp. pepper
1	tsp. lemon juice		

Combine mayonnaise, sour cream, dill, lemon juice and seasonings. Mix well. Cover and refrigerate several hours for flavors to blend. Brush salmon steaks with additional lemon juice and grill over medium coals until just done. Serve with dill sauce.

Wallace Brandt
Concord, California

SALMON LOAF

1 pint canned salmon
2 cups soft bread crumbs
1/3 cup onion, finely minced
1/4 cup milk
1/2 tsp. ground ginger
   dash of white and black pepper
2 eggs
2 T. minced fresh parsley
1 T. lemon juice
1/4 tsp. dried dill weed
1/4 tsp. garlic powder

Drain salmon, leaving 2 tablespoons of the liquid. Flake the salmon, then combine with the liquid and the remaining ingredients. Mix well and shape into a loaf. Place in greased baking pan. Bake for 30 minutes at 350°.

Ron Jurgovan
Posen, Illinois

SMOKED SALMON OR STEELHEAD

salmon or steelhead
1 cup brown sugar
½ cup white sugar
1 T. seasoned salt
½ tsp. garlic salt
rock salt

Steve Shanks, Don's grandson

Cut the fish into 1½ inch chunks. Mix the sugars, seasoned salt and garlic salt together to form a salty/sweet combination. Lay the fish chunks, skin side down, in a covered container (do not use wood or aluminum). Rub the salty/sweet mixture into the fish, and then sprinkle a light layer of rock salt over. Refrigerate for 6-7 hours. The fish will make its own brine. Remove from the refrigerator and rinse in cold water. Let the fish dry for 1 hour.

Smoke the fish for 3 to 4 hours, using alder or any other hard wood chips. Let the fish cool after smoking. The flavor is best if fish is left to set for a day. The fish will last for 2 to 3 weeks in the refrigerator.

Don Shanks
Everett, Washington

Salmon Bake with Cheese and Asparagus

- 2 fillets of land-lock salmon or lake trout (10-12 oz. each)
- 8 spears asparagus
- 1 pint heavy cream
- 2 6-oz. cans shrimp, drained
  salt
  pepper
- 1/2 cup Cheddar cheese
  bread crumbs

Rinse and remove the skin from the fillets. Roll 4 spears of asparagus in each fillet, and secure with toothpicks. Simmer the fillets in a skillet over medium heat with the cream and 1 can of shrimp, until the fillets are flaky but not falling apart. Remove from the heat and add the second can of shrimp. Sprinkle the fillets with salt, pepper, the cheese and the bread crumbs. Bake at 350° until the cheese melts and the tops brown.

Robert A. Roske
East Hampton, Massachusetts

Orange Salmon

- 1 king or silver salmon fillet (3-5 lbs.)
- 1/2 can orange juice concentrate
- 1/4 soy sauce

Combine the orange juice concentrate and soy sauce and stir until blended. Lay the fillet on a foil-covered baking sheet and pour mixture over the fillet. Put in the refrigerator for 1/2 hour. Brush the excess sauce off with a basting brush. Grill fillet, with or without foil, basting with the extra sauce.

Dave Peterson
Juneau, Alaska

BACKYARD BARBECUE SALMON

1	salmon (can also use trout) whole, dressed
6-8	strips bacon
2	lemons, sliced
½	cup butter, chopped
2	small onions, cut into wedges

Put the ¼ cup butter and half of onions inside the salmon. Wrap the bacon strips around the salmon and lay it on foil. Add the remaining onion, butter, and 1 sliced lemon. Wrap the foil tightly around salmon, and barbecue until done. Serve remaining lemon with cooked salmon.

John G. Daniels
Springfield, Oregon

SALMON MONTEREY

	salmon steaks
½	lb. crab meat (can use imitation)
½	lb. small bay shrimp
6	green onions, chopped
12	black olives, sliced
	cayenne pepper
	sour cream
	shredded Monterey Jack cheese

Mix together the crab, shrimp, onions, olives, cayenne pepper to taste, and enough sour cream to bind everything together. Broil the salmon steaks until done, and then top with the crab and shrimp mixture and the cheese. Microwave for 1 minute per steak to melt cheese.

Harold Eurich
Colfax, California

GRILLED TERIYAKI SALMON

- 4 salmon steaks, about 1" thick
- 1 cup teriyaki sauce/marinade
- 3 cloves fresh garlic, chopped
- 1 tsp. honey

In a large bowl, mix the teriyaki sauce, garlic and honey. Soak the salmon steaks for 6 hours, or overnight for best flavor. Place the steaks on a hot charcoal grill, and cook 7-10 minutes on each side. Remove the steaks, and serve hot or cold with a fresh garden salad or other cold salad.

Ronald Meltreder
Freehold, New Jersey

POACHED SALMON FILLETS OR STEAKS

- 2 salmon fillets or salmon steaks, 1" thick
- 2 T. butter or margarine
- 1/2 cup white wine or Worcestershire sauce
- 2 large cloves garlic, minced
- 1/4 cup fresh lemon juice
- 1 tsp. lemon zest
- 1/4 cup fresh dill, or 1 T. dried dill
- 1 tsp. fresh thyme
  water

Melt the butter or margarine in a frying pan over medium heat. Add the wine or Worcestershire sauce, garlic, lemon juice and zest, dill and thyme, stirring constantly. Add the salmon and water, if needed, to make 1/4 inch liquid in the pan. Cover and poach until the fish flakes, turning once if desired. Serve fish with sauce spooned over it.

You may use other fresh herbs, if you wish. You may use other firm fish such as haddock, cod, halibut, striped bass or lake trout.

Mrs. C. E. Lugmbuhl
Agawam, Massachusetts

BROILED STEELHEAD SALMON IN LIME AND CILANTRO MARINADE

- 1 lb. steelhead salmon fillets (skin on)
- 1/4 cup chopped fresh cilantro
- 1/2 cup fresh lime juice
- 1 tsp. salt
- 1/4 tsp. ground white pepper
- 2 cups salad oil

Cut the fish into 3-6 ounce pieces. Mix the other ingredients in a large bowl, and marinate the fish in the mixture overnight in the refrigerator. Preheat the broiler, place the fillets skin-side-up on well-buttered pieces of foil on the broiler pan. Spoon on the marinade. Place the pan 4 inches under the broiler and cook 6-8 minutes, or until meat is opaque. Do not turn.

Note: Having the fish skin-side-up prevents, it from drying out as much.

Manuel and Karen Silva
Cupertino, California

FISH BOATS

1 can pink salmon	1 tsp. lemon juice
4 oz. small package of soft processed cheese	pinch of salt
	5 T. mayonnaise
3 small sweet pickles	2 sourdough rolls

Drain the salmon well, remove the bones, and flake into small bite-size pieces. Dice the cheese and pickles and mix well. Toss with lemon juice, salt and mayonnaise. Chill in the refrigerator for 30 minutes.

Cut the top off of the sourdough rolls and remove the center. Fill the rolls with the salmon mixture; bake with the tops of the rolls off at 425° for 20-25 minutes or until the cheese melts and is light brown.

Scott Green
Salt Lake City, Utah

Seared Salmon with a Warm Raspberry Vinaigrette (Supreme de Saumon Sauté aux Vinaigrette de Framboises)

1 salmon fillets (6-8 oz.), skinless
2 T. raspberry vinegar
2 T. olive oil
1 small clove garlic, crushed and pressed
  squeeze of lemon juice
1 T. olive oil
  salt
  pepper
3 fresh raspberries
2 fresh mint leaves

To make the vinaigrette, combine the raspberry vinegar, 2 tablespoons of olive oil, garlic and lemon juice in a mixing bowl. Whisk together and set to one side.

Heat the 1 tablespoon of olive oil in a skillet until it begins to smoke. Season the salmon with salt and pepper and carefully place it in the skillet. Allow the salmon to brown. Keep turning the salmon, while gradually lowering the heat, until cooked. Remove the salmon from the skillet and place it on a plate. Add the vinaigrette to the hot skillet. Let it come to a fast boil and pour it over the salmon. Garnish with the raspberries and the mint leaves. Serve immediately.

Mike Davis
Portland, Oregon

Bob Keeney

BOB'S SMOKED SALMON OR STEELHEAD

   salmon or steelhead fillets, skinned
1 gallon water
1 cup brown sugar
1 cup pickling salt
1 T. ground thyme
1 T. whole allspice berries
2 bay leaves
   black pepper
   seasoned salt
   red pepper seasoning (optional)

Boil all ingredients, except the fish, pepper, seasoned salt and red pepper, to form the brine. Stirring constantly. Let it cool. Soak the fillets in brine overnight. Smoke fillets with hickory wood chunks, according to your smoker's directions, turning halfway through cooking time. Season both sides of fillets with the black pepper, seasoned salt, and red pepper seasoning.

Bob Keeney
Brighton, Michigan

SALMON STEAKS YUM YUM

        salmon steaks
        sliced onions
¹/₂   cup raisins
¹/₂   cup brown sugar (light or dark)
        fresh squeezed lemon juice

Place the salmon in a skillet on a layer of onions with enough water to slightly cover the fish. Add the raisins and brown sugar. Simmer until the salmon turns light in color, 15-20 minutes. Add the lemon juice while the fish is cooking. The sauce will have a golden color.

Serve with a vegetable.

Arthur Sweatt
Laconia, New Hampshire

SALMON BAKE WITH PECAN CRUNCH COATING

4   salmon fillets, (4-6 oz.)   ¹/₄   cup finely chopped pecans
2   T. Dijon mustard   2   tsp. chopped parsley
2   T. unsalted   salt
       butter, melted   black pepper
2   tsp. honey   lemon wedges
¹/₄ cup fresh bread
       crumbs

Mix the mustard, butter and honey together in a small bowl; set aside. Mix together the fresh bread crumbs, pecans and chopped parsley; set aside. Season each fillet with salt and pepper. Place the fish on a lightly greased baking sheet, brushing each fillet with mustard-honey mixture. Pat the top of each fillet with the bread crumb mixture. Bake at 450° for 10 minutes per inch of thickness, measured at the thickest part, or until the salmon just flakes when tested with a fork.

Serve with lemon wedges.

Eugene Cord
Chattanooga, Tennessee

BAKED SALMON PACKETS WITH DILL

1¹/₂ lbs. salmon fillets
2 T. margarine
1 tsp. dried dill
freshly ground black pepper

Place fillets on 1 or more large rectangular pieces of foil. Top with pats of margarine, and season with dill and pepper. Bring the longer ends of the foil together and double fold; fold in the 2 remaining sides, making sure all edges are well-sealed. Place foil packets on a baking sheet and bake at 425° for 10 minutes.

Rick Washousky
Clarence, New York

CANNED SALMON

skinless salmon fillets, cut into 1¹/₂" cubes
¹/₄ tsp. salt
1 T. vinegar
¹/₄ tsp. oil
1 T. ketchup or barbecue sauce

Fill a pint-size canning jar with fillets to within 1 inch of the top. Combine the rest of the ingredients, add to jar and seal the jar. Use a pressure cooker, according the your cooker's directions, to process salmon. Or, using your conventional oven, heat jar in pot of water to 375°, then turn heat down to 225° and cook the jar for 3 hours. Put the jar on a cooling rack and let stand until the seal is made.

Now you are ready to use the fish in your favorite recipe for salmon patties, salmon salad, salmon cheese ball, etc.

Robert Saros
Mishawaka, Indiana

SMOKED SALMON PASTA

8   oz. thinly sliced smoked salmon
8   large mushrooms, sliced
1½   tomatoes, diced
4   green onions, chopped
2   T. clarified butter
    salt
    white pepper
½   T. chopped dill weed
1½   cups heavy cream
    Parmesan cheese
    spinach fettuccine, cooked

Sauté the vegetables in butter for 1 minute over medium heat. Season to taste with the salt and pepper. Add the cream and bring to a boil. Stir in just enough cheese to thicken the sauce. Add the salmon and simmer for 1 minute. Toss mixture with the spinach fettuccine.

Harold Eurich
Colfax, California

SALMON FILLETS SWEDISH STYLE

4   salmon fillets   pepper
    fresh dill   fine bread crumbs
1   egg, beaten   butter
    salt

Line a baking dish with 3 inches of fresh dill. Lay the salmon fillets on the dill, skin side down. Brush the fillets with beaten egg; add salt and pepper to taste. Sprinkle with a light layer of bread crumbs. Dot with butter, and bake in a very hot (490°) oven for 25-30 minutes, basting with melted butter.

Serve with small boiled potatoes, creamed spinach and bèarnaise sauce.

Frank H. Brzoticky
Arvada, Colorado

SALMON OR LAKE TROUT STEAKS OR FILLETS

      salmon, lake trout, or trout fish steaks or fillets
¼ lemon per steak, squeezed, including the pulp
¼ orange per steak, squeezed, including the pulp
      pinch of garlic powder
      pinch of salt
      pinch of lemon pepper, or black pepper to taste
      melted butter, olive oil, or cooking oil

Rinse the steaks or fillets in cold water, drain and pat dry. Brush with butter or oil. Sprinkle with lemon and orange juices, a little garlic powder, salt and pepper to taste (you can add onion powder, if desired). Place the fish in a foil-lined baking dish and bake in a 350° oven for 15-20 minutes. Remove from the oven. Turn over the steaks or fillets; sprinkle with more salt, pepper and garlic powder; and bake for another 10-15, minutes or until the fish flakes easily with a fork.

To change the taste, add a little brown sugar before cooking.

Serve with steamed rice and vegetables. Serve 1-2 steaks or fillets per person (don't skimp).

Manuel G. Martinez
Ogden, Utah

CREAMY SALMON AND CHEESE SOUP

1½ lbs. salmon, fresh or canned, boiled and flaked
1 cup chopped onion
1 cup chopped celery
7 T. butter
7 T. flour
7 cups milk
2 tsp. soy sauce
8-10 slices American cheese
2 cans carrots, drained
2 cans peas, drained
1 cup chopped cooked potato
1 tsp. salt

In a large pot, sauté the onion and celery in the butter until clear and tender. Stir in the flour and blend well. Stir in the milk and soy sauce, cooking on medium-high heat until thickened. Add the cheese and simmer until the cheese is blended in. Add the salmon and remaining ingredients and simmer for 15 minutes, stirring occasionally.

Harry W. Clontz

Serve with oyster crackers or saltines.

Harry W. Clontz
Brockway, Pennsylvania

SMOKED SALMON SPREAD

1½   lbs. smoked salmon
  2   tsp. finely chopped celery
  1   T. finely chopped sweet pickle
  1   garlic clove, minced
  2   T. chopped parsley
  2   tsp. minced onion
1½   cups mayonnaise
  1   T. mustard
       dash of Worcestershire sauce

Remove the skin and bones from the fish and flake well. Mix all ingredients together and chill for 1 hour before serving.

Ron Jurgovan
Posen, Illinois

BAKED CHEESE AND MUSHROOM FILLETS

3-4   lbs. salmon or trout fillets
  ¼   cup pickling salt
  ¼   cup dark brown sugar
  1   cup grated cheese
  1   can condensed cream of mushroom soup
  ½   cup white wine or sherry
  1   small can of any type of mushrooms, drained
       salt
       pepper

Dissolve the pickling salt and brown sugar in 4 cups of cold water. Soak the fillets in the brine for 30 minutes, then rinse in cold water and towel dry. Cut the fillets into 4-6 ounce portions and arrange in a baking dish. In a bowl, combine cheese, soup, wine and mushrooms. Pour the mixture over the fillets. Bake at 375° for 25-30 minutes.

Ron Jurgoven
Posen, Illinois

BRAISED SALMON, TROUT, OR WALLEYE PARISIENNE

3 lbs. salmon, trout or walleye fillets
2 tsp. salt
1 tsp. crushed peppercorns
1 tsp. ground nutmeg
   thin-sliced bacon
   white wine or dry sherry
1 T. chopped mushrooms
1 T. tomato paste
3 T. heavy cream, scalded
2 T. butter
   lemon
   parsley

Clean, wipe and trim the fish. Rub with salt, pepper and nutmeg. Wrap the fish with bacon strips and place in a well-buttered pan. Add enough wine or sherry to nearly cover the fish. Top with mushrooms. Cover with buttered parchment paper.

Cook the fish in a 350° oven for 30 minutes, basting occasionally. Remove the paper and bake for another 5 minutes. Place on a hot plate and keep warm.

To make the sauce: Simmer the liquid from the baking dish. Add the tomato paste and cream and cook for 5 minutes. Add the butter and additional seasonings, if necessary. Pour a little sauce over the fish and garnish with the lemon and parsley.

Roger R. Walker
Selby, South Dakota

CAJUN BLACKENING SPICE

1½ cups ground black pepper
½ cup cayenne pepper
1 cup white pepper
1 cup sweet basil, dried
¾ cup paprika
¼ cup garlic powder
½ cup onion powder
1 cup salt
¼ cup ground thyme
¼ cup chili powder

The cup size can be varied (i.e. the scoop from the bulk foods department) as long as the proportions are kept the same. Rub on salmon fillets or steaks before grilling or pan-frying.

Scott. D. Stevens
Calgary, Alberta

BAKED FISH FOR LAZY FISHERMEN

salmon or trout fillets
mayonnaise
garlic salt
white pepper
black pepper
parsley flakes

Cut fillets into 8-oz portions and spread mayonnaise on both sides. Lay fish on aluminum foil. Sprinkle with salt, peppers, parsley, and any other spice that is within arm's reach. Bake at 400° for 20 minutes, or until fish flakes with a fork. Place under the broiler for 2-3 minutes for a golden brown color.

Ron Jurgoven
Posen, Illinois

BLACKENED SALMON WITH CREOLE SAUCE

4   salmon fillets (5-7 oz. each), skinned and deboned
4   tsp. canola oil
4   tsp. Cajun blackening spice
¼   cup canola oil
1   medium-large onion, chopped or sliced
1   cup or can sliced mushrooms
1   small can diced tomatoes

Heat a cast-iron frying pan until it is very hot—just about smoking. On a plate, lightly coat the salmon with the 4 teaspoons of oil, less is better. Then sprinkle the Cajun spice on fillets until both sides are lightly covered. Place the salmon in the pan and stand back. There will be a lot of smoke as the oil and spices sear and their flavorful smoke infuses the salmon. Turn the fish over only once, after 3-5 minutes, depending on the thickness of the fish.

Remove the salmon to a plate and use the same pan for the sauce. Let the pan cool to medium and then add the ¼ cup of oil, then onion, and mushrooms; fry until they start to brown. Add the tomatoes, heat to boiling and season with more Cajun spice.

Spoon the sauce over the salmon and serve.

Note: I have used the Cajun blackening spice to season many different types of fish, including salmon, halibut, roughy, trout, tuna, walleye, shrimp and scallops.

Scott. D. Stevens
Calgary, Alberta

KENAI SMOKED SALMON

salmon
1/2 cup canning/
pickling salt
1 T. black
pepper
1 T. ground
allspice

Mix all ingredients, except fish, to form a brine. Set aside. Fillet and clean the fish, then cut fillets into 1½-2 inch strips and soak in rock salt (non-iodized) and water (1 cup of salt to 1 gallon of water) for 20 minutes. Rinse and blot the salmon strips dry.

Roll the strips in brine mixture, place in plastic

Guy G. Cordeiro

bags, tie securely, and place bags in refrigerator. Turn the bags over every hour for four hours until the skin is wrinkly. (You can brine up to 12 hours.) Rinse the brine off of the fish and pat dry. Place the strips on smoker racks and air-dry overnight, or until there is a glaze on the fish. Put the racks in smokers for 6-10 hours (depending on thickness).

Guy G. Cordeiro
Anchorage, AK

SYLVESTER'S SMOKED SALMON

       salmon
   1   cup water
   ½   cup soy sauce
   ⅓   tsp. citric acid
   ½   cup brown sugar
   ½   tsp. dried thyme
   3   T. parsley
   1   tsp. lemon pepper
       olive oil

Combine all the ingredients, except the fish and the olive oil, in a
saucepan. Bring to a boil, and boil for 1 minute; let marinade cool.
Cut the fish into serving size pieces and soak in the marinade overnight.
Drain marinade from fish and pat dry. Rub the fish with the oil and then
smoke it. I use briquettes for heat, and when they are good and hot,
I add some applewood or vine maple that has been soaked in water.

Sylvester
Forest Grove, Oregon

DILL SMOKED FISH

5-6 lbs. salmon or
     trout fillets
  1 large onion, quartered
  1 T. dried dill weed
  2 T. dried parsley
  3 cloves garlic
  2 shallots
  1 2" piece of ginger
$^3/_4$ cup soy sauce
$^1/_2$ cup red or white wine
$^1/_2$ cup brown sugar
  1 T. salt

  1 T. onion powder
  2 whole cloves
  2 bay leaves
  1 tsp. garlic powder
  3 lbs. hickory or other
     wood chips, soaked in
     water overnight

To make brine: Combine onion, dill, parsley, garlic, shallots and ginger in a blender or food processor and purée. Pour into a large glass bowl (must be big enough to hold the fish). Add remaining ingredients, except fish and woodchips, and mix well. Add fish and just enough water to cover. Refrigerate 2-3 days, turning several times.

To smoke: Prepare barbecue by heaping briquettes on one side of the grill (start with about 30 for a large grill). Ignite and burn the coals until they glow and gray ash forms. Set drip pan opposite of briquettes. Remove fish from brine and wipe dry. Pile wood chips over briquettes. Set cooking grid in place and coat side over drip pan with non-stick vegetable spray.

Immediately place fish over drip pan, and cover barbecue. Leave one or two vents open to let the smoke escape. Smoke until fish flakes when tested with a fork, allowing about 8 minutes per pound. (Time will depend on weather; if temperature is cold, it can take up to 2 hours or longer.) Add coals, as necessary, if briquettes begin to burn down.

Transfer fish to platter and let cool. Cover and refrigerate until 1 hour before you are ready to serve.

Bob Houston
Fremont, California

GRILLED SHARK STEAK WITH KEY LIME MAYONNAISE

4 shark steaks (about 5 oz. each)
¼ cup extra-virgin olive oil
¼ cup Key West lime juice
2 T. lime cilantro seasoning or fresh cilantro
2 T. jalapeño pepper jelly
1 tsp. hot pepper sauce

Key Lime Mayonnaise:

½ cup mayonnaise
2 T. Key West lime juice
1 T. lime cilantro seasoning or chopped cilantro
3 T. chopped fresh dill

Wipe the fish with a damp cloth and pat dry. Prepare the marinade by combining the olive oil, ¼ cup lime juice, 2 tablespoon lime cilantro seasoning, jalapeño jelly and pepper hot sauce in a shallow glass bowl. Add the shark steaks and turn to coat well. Cover and let them marinate at room temperature for 30 minutes.

Cook the fish on a lightly greased grill over medium-high heat, until the fish is opaque all the way through or just slightly translucent in the center, about 3-5 minutes.

Combine the ingredients for the key lime mayonnaise and serve with the fish.

Leo G. J. Seffelaar
Broadview, Saskatchewan

WOK-COOKED SHRIMP WITH VEGETABLES

shrimp, peeled and deveined
summer squash, sliced
mushrooms, sliced
onions, sliced
bell pepper, sliced
Italian dressing
Worcestershire sauce
garlic powder
black pepper·
seasoning salt
olive oil spray

Marinate the shrimp and vegetables in Italian dressing with a dash of Worcestershire sauce for 1 hour. Sprinkle with garlic powder, pepper and seasoned salt.

Spray a wok with olive oil and place over medium heat. Remove the shrimp and the vegetables from the marinade with a slotted spoon and place in the wok. Sauté until the vegetables and shrimp are done.

Note: Chicken can be used in place of the shrimp. The vegetables may be done alone as an accompaniment to steak or other seafood.

Gary Crim
Bessemer, Alabama

BAKED WHOLE SNAPPER

	whole red snapper	coarse ground black pepper
	lemon wedges	Greek seasoning
2-3	T. white wine	garlic powder
	olive oil	seasoning salt
	lemon pepper	green onion, slivered

Score the whole snapper 3 or 4 times on each side. Squeeze the lemon wedges into the fish cavity. Add the wine and then marinate for 30-40 minutes. Drain the excess lemon juice and wine from fish. Coat the inside and outside of the fish with olive oil and then sprinkle with the spices to taste. The green onion slivers may be placed inside the score marks before baking. Bake at 350° for 15-20 minutes, until fish flakes.

Gary Crim
Bessemer, Alabama

GRILLED RED SNAPPER

	red snapper steaks	coarse ground black pepper
2	T. white wine	oregano
2	tsp. lemon juice	Greek seasoning
	olive oil	garlic powder
	lemon pepper	seasoning salt

Marinate the fish steaks in the wine and the lemon juice for 30-40 minutes. Drain and coat lightly in olive oil. Sprinkle the remaining ingredients to taste on both sides of the fish. Grill on medium heat, until the fish flakes, turning steaks a couple of times.

For king mackerel, tuna and swordfish steaks, add tomato sauce to the marinade. Season the fish and then marinate again for another 20-30 minutes.

Gary Crim
Bessemer, Alabama

SNAPPER WITH A WHITE SAUCE

1-2 lbs. red snapper fillets
1/2 tsp. salt
1/2 tsp. pepper
1/4 tsp. garlic powder
3/4 cup water
4 T. butter or margarine
2 T. minced green onion, the white parts only
1/4 cup all-purpose flour
1 cup milk
1/2 tsp. dried oregano leaves
1/4 cup Cheddar cheese
cayenne pepper to taste

Sprinkle the fish with salt, pepper and garlic powder and place it in a single layer in a buttered baking dish. Pour the water around the fillets; bake, uncovered, at 400° for 10 minutes. Drain liquid from dish, reserving 1/3 of it. Set liquid and fish aside.

Melt the butter in a skillet and sauté the onion quickly. Stir in the flour and cook and stir over moderate heat until it is golden brown. Whisk in the reserved liquid, the milk and oregano. Cook until the sauce thickens, then season with salt to taste. Pour the sauce over the fish and sprinkle with cheese and cayenne pepper. Bake at 400° for 10-15 minutes.

Willie Monterio
Hoquiam, Washington

CRABMEAT-STUFFED SOLE

4 3-oz. sole fillets (can also use flounder or
  orange roughy)
3 tsp. reduced-calorie margarine, divided
¹/₄ cup chopped green onions
¹/₄ lb. fresh lump crabmeat or
  imitation crabmeat, drained
¹/₂ cup soft French-bread crumbs
¹/₄ cup chopped fresh parsley
¹/₄ cup plain nonfat yogurt
1 tsp. dried oregano
1 tsp. lemon juice
¹/₄ cup grated Romano or Parmesan cheese

Coat a small nonstick skillet with non-stick cooking spray and add
1 teaspoon margarine. Melt the margarine over medium-high heat.
Add the green onions and sauté for 1 minute. Add the crabmeat, bread
crumbs, parsley, yogurt, oregano, and lemon juice and stir well. Spoon
¹/₄ cup crabmeat mixture into the center of each fillet and roll up,
starting at the narrow end. Secure with wooden toothpicks. Place the
rolls seam-side down in an 8 inch square baking dish coated with
cooking spray. Brush evenly with 2 tsp. of melted margarine.

Bake, uncovered, at 350° for 10 minutes. Sprinkle the cheese evenly over
the fish and bake an additional 10 minutes, or until fish flakes easily when
tested with a fork. Transfer to a serving platter and serve immediately.

This dish goes great with glazed baby carrots and a green salad.

Leo G. J. Seffelaar
Broadview, Saskatchewan

Smothered Sole

2   lbs. Pacific sole fillets (may also use halibut,
      cod, perch, or snapper)
1   tsp. seasoned salt
1/2 cup chopped onion
1/2 cup chopped green pepper
4   small tomatoes, thinly sliced
1   lemon, thinly sliced
1/2 cup white wine
1/4 cup oil

Place the fillets in a greased 2-quart casserole dish. Sprinkle with the
seasoned salt, onion and green pepper. Arrange the tomato slices and
then the lemon slices over all. Combine the wine and the oil and pour
over the fish. Bake at 400°
for 20-25 minutes, basting twice.

Leo G. J. Seffelaar
Broadview, Saskatchewan

Baked Creamed Sturgeon

sturgeon   bacon strips
baking soda   cream
salt   butter
pepper

Place the fish in a large pan. Pour boiling water over it, then scrape the
skin with a knife until all the black and shine is scraped off. Bring a kettle
of water with soda and salt added to a boil. Drop chunks of the fish into
kettle but do not let water return to a boil. Watch closely; as soon as the
skin starts to loosen, take the fish out of the water and remove the skin.

Season fish with salt and pepper on all sides and place it in a roaster, belly
down. Put strips of bacon over the fish and pour cream and butter over
the fish. Bake until golden brown. Set oven at about 425° for the first
15 minutes, then reduce the heat to 350° until done, about 5 minutes.

Norma Blank
Shawano, Wisconsin

"STURGEON STEVE'S" STURGEON CHOWDER

- 3 lbs. sturgeon, filleted and cut into 1/2" cubes
- 1 lb. bacon, fat trimmed off and chopped
- 2 large onions, chopped
- 6 stalks celery, diced
- 2 carrots, peeled and sliced
- 1 green bell pepper, chopped
- 1 red bell pepper, chopped
- 1 whole garlic bulb, peeled and chopped
- 12 potatoes, peeled and cubed
- 1/2 cup corn kernels
- 2 jalapeños, sliced
- 1 T. salt
- 1 T. pepper
- 1 tsp. dried oregano
- 1 tsp. dried basil
- 8 cups fish stock, chicken stock, or water
- 4 cups half-and-half
- 1 cup instant mashed potatoes (optional, to be used as a thickener)
- 1 tsp. parsley, chopped fresh or dried

Brown the bacon in a large stock pot. Add the onions, celery, carrots, bell peppers and garlic. Sauté for about 15 minutes, stirring occasionally. Add the potatoes, corn, jalapeños and spices. Just cover contents of pot with the stock, adding more water if needed.

Cover and boil until the potatoes are done, stirring occasionally. Reduce heat, add half-and-half and fish (fish turns white when done). Stirring occasionally, add instant potatoes to achieve desired thickness. Let chowder cool slightly, garnish with parsley, and serve with french bread.

Note: Any white fish fillets may be substituted for the sturgeon. Soup stock can be made from boiled and strained fish carcasses.

Tracy Stevenson
Portland, Oregon

GRILLED SWORDFISH AND VEGGIE KABOBS

1½ lbs. swordfish, cut into 1" cubes
4   T. lemon herb spice
8   large white button mushrooms
2   medium zucchini, sliced ½" thick

Sprinkle lemon herb spice evenly over swordfish. Refrigenerate for ½ hour. Skewer the fish with the mushrooms and the zucchini pieces. Grill or broil the kabobs for 4-5 minutes on each side, until fish is cooked throughout.

Rick Washousky
Clarence, New York

SWORDFISH STEAKS

2   lbs. swordfish steaks
½   tsp. salt
     pepper to taste
2   cups herb-seasoned stuffing mix
12   pimentos-stuffed green olives, sliced
1⅓   cups hot water
4-5 slices bacon, cut in half

Place the fish in a well-greased, shallow baking dish. Season the fish with salt and pepper. Combine the stuffing, olives and water; spread mixture over the steaks. Top with the bacon. Bake, uncovered, at 350° for 30-35 minutes, or until the fish flakes easily when tested with a fork.

Arthur Sweatt
Laconia, New Hampshire

STUFFED POOR MAN'S LOBSTER

- 4 skinless tataug or sea bass fillets (1 lb. each)
- 1 1-lb. pkg. artificial crabmeat
- ½ cup Italian bread crumbs
- 1 egg, well beaten
- ¼ cup mayonnaise
- ¼ tsp. seafood seasoning
- 2 T. butter or margarine
- ¼ cup flour
- ¾ cup whole milk
- ¼ cup butter or margarine, melted

Rinse the fillets thoroughly with cold water. Shred the artificial crabmeat and place in a bowl. In a separate bowl, combine the bread crumbs, egg, mayonnaise and seasoning; mix completely. Melt the 2 tablespoon butter or margarine in a saucepan over low heat. Stir in the flour in until it forms a paste. Add the milk and continue cooking until it thickens. Remove from the heat and add the artificial crabmeat; mix lightly.

Place the fillets on a broiler pan that has been sprayed with non-stick cooking spray. Cover the fish with a 2 inch layer of the crab mix, top with bread crumb mixture, and baste with butter. Place in a preheated 350° oven for 20 minutes, basting at 5 minute intervals.

Serve with a small bowl of garlic butter with each plate.

Lucien J. Beaulieu
North Grosvenordale, Connecticut

FILLET OF TROUT
WITH CRAB MEAT AND LEMON BUTTER BRANDY SAUCE

  2 large trout fillets, boned with the skin on

Marinade:
- 1/2 tsp. fresh rosemary
- 1/2 tsp. fresh fennel seed
- 1/2 tsp. fresh celery seed
- 1/2 tsp. fresh marjoram
- 1/2 tsp. fresh sweet basil
- 1/4 cup Rhine flur wine
- 1/2 tsp. soy sauce
- dried minced onion to taste
- 1/2 tsp. fresh lemon juice

Flour coating:
- 1/4 cup flour
- 1/2 tsp. onion salt
- 1/2 tsp. garlic salt

Filling:
- 1/4 cup flacked crab meat

John's lemon butter brandy sauce:
- 1 T. butter
- 1 T. fresh lemon juice
- 2 oz. brandy
- parsley for color

Prepare the marinade by chopping the herbs to form a paste, then add the wine, soy sauce, dried onion and lemon juice. In a dish, place the fish skin-side-up in the marinade, cover it, and refrigerate for 1-2 hours. Remove from the refrigerator and reserve the marinade.

Rub the fish skin with olive oil. Mix the flour, onion salt and garlic salt. Cover the skin side only with flour coating.

Wrap the fish in foil by placing the foil on an angle. Place one fillet, skin-side-down, on foil; top with crab. Top with second fillet, skin-side -up.

Wrap the foil around the fish leaving the top portion of the foil open; add reserved marinade until full. Close the foil tightly.

To make the butter sauce: Place the sauce ingredients together in a pan and boil to make a glaze. Keep warm.

Broil or grill foil packet about 3-5 minutes per side. Remove from the heat and top with the lemon butter brandy sauce.

Serve with rice, lemon wedges and asparagus.

WHOLE TROUT WRAPPED IN SMOKED BACON AND ROSEMARY

1	10-12" per person, dressed, whole (any freshwater trout may be used)
1	clove garlic, minced
1	bay leaf
1	tsp. fresh ground black pepper
1	T. olive oil
	thin-sliced bacon
1	bunch fresh rosemary
	juice of 1 whole lemon
1	T. fresh chopped parsley

Rub the inside of the trout with the garlic, bay leaf and black pepper. Brush the outside with the oil and wrap the fish in bacon (evenly and overlapping the bacon around the fish). Place the branches of rosemary on broiler pan and top with fish; broil fish approximately 3-4 minutes per side.

When cooked, transfer the whole fish, discarding the rosemary, to a clean plate. Sprinkle with the fresh squeezed lemon juice and the parsley.

John Putluck
Salt Lake City, Utah

PAN-FRIED TROUT

  3   pan-dressed trout (10-12 oz. each)
  1   egg, beaten
  2   T. water
$^3/_4$ cup finely crushed saltine crackers
$^1/_2$ tsp. salt
$^1/_2$ tsp. pepper
     cooking oil for frying

In a shallow dish, beat the egg and water together. In another bowl, combine the crushed crackers, salt and pepper. Dip the fish in the egg and then roll in the crackers. Fry the fish in the oil until brown.

Dylon Bjorgaard
Newfolden, Minnesota

HAMBURGER-STUFFED TROUT

  1   trout, preferably wild
$^1/_2$ lb. ground beef
     garlic salt
     lemon pepper
  4   slices of bacon

Mix the ground beef and spices of your choice (garlic salt, lemon pepper, etc.). Clean the trout and stuff with the beef mixture. Wrap the bacon around the fish and secure with toothpicks. Cook at 325° for 1 hour, until the skin starts to peel or the flesh starts to flake off. Garnish with fresh parsley.

Kevin LaSalle
Gooding, Idaho

STUFFED TROUT

1	8-oz. whole, dressed trout per serving
6	fresh mushrooms, sliced
2	medium onions, chopped
¼	cup chopped parsley
4	T. butter
1¼	cups bread crumbs
	pinch of sage
¼	tsp. onion salt
¼	tsp. garlic salt
¼	tsp. celery salt
	fresh ground pepper
	melted butter

Wash the trout in cold water and pat dry. Sauté the mushrooms, onions and parsley in butter until the onions are soft. Toss the onion mixture with the bread crumbs. Add the sage, onion salt, garlic salt, celery salt and pepper to taste. Stuff the trout cavities with crumb mixture and place in a buttered baking pan. Brush the trout with melted butter. Bake at 400° for 20-25 minutes. Place any extra stuffing in a baking dish, cover, and place in the oven for 20 minutes before serving. Serve hot.

Scott Green
Salt Lake City, Utah

TROUT OR SALMON PATTIES

1	lb. trout fillets	milk
	lemon juice	crackers
1	egg	margarine or butter
1	onion, chopped	salt and pepper

Bake the trout wrapped in aluminum foil with a little lemon juice. Shred meat and remove any bones. Mix the egg, onion, milk and crackers with trout to form mixture that will pack together; form patties. Fry patties in margarine or butter in a skillet until brown. Season with salt and pepper.

Ray E. Mellott
Findlay, Ohio

Pan-Fried Brook Trout

4   brook trout, cleaned with head and tails left on
2   T. flour
     salt
7   T. butter, divided
3   T. oil
2   T. lemon juice
2   T. minced chives

Rinse fish under cold water and then pat dry with paper towels. Dust with flour and sprinkle with salt. Melt 3 tablespoon of butter with oil in a large skillet. Fry the fish over medium-high heat. Brown for about 4 minutes on each side. Melt the remaining butter with the lemon juice and chives in a small pan. Place the fish on a platter and pour lemon-butter over it.

Gary Wright
Greely, Colorado

Trout Philadelphia Style

4   trout fillets
1   onion, chopped
     olive oil
1   clove garlic, chopped
½   cup sliced mushrooms
1   tsp. Worcestershire sauce
½   cup chopped green pepper

1   cup beer
2   T. lemon juice
4   pats of margarine
     salt
     pepper
1   tsp. Mombassa (African cayenne) or cayenne pepper
4   strips bacon, cooked

Rinse the fish well, coat with olive oil, and put in a baking dish along with the onion, garlic, mushrooms, Worcestershire sauce, green pepper, beer and lemon juice. Put the pats of margarine on top of the fish, and salt and pepper fish to taste. Marinate for 3 hours. Sprinkle cayenne on top of the fish. Bake at 350°, basting until fish is almost done. Lay the bacon over the fish and finish baking, until fish flakes.

Greg Kliniewski
Philadelphia, Pennsylvania

WILD RICE STUFFED TROUT

4	16" drawn trout (1/2 lb. per person)
1	cup uncooked wild rice
2 1/2	cups hot water
1	tsp. salt
1/3	cup chopped water chestnuts
1/4	cup chopped green onions
1	T. chopped stuffed green olives
3	T. butter

Rinse and drain the rice. Combine the rice, water and salt in a 3-quart saucepan. Heat to boiling, stirring once or twice. Reduce the heat, cover, and simmer until the rice is tender, about 45 minutes. Check the rice to prevent sticking and add more water if needed. Set aside.

Heat the oven to 375°, and grease a 13 x 9 inch baking pan. In a small skillet, cook and stir the water chestnuts, green onions and olives in butter over medium heat for 2 minutes. Stir in the rice.

Put the trout in prepared pan; stuff trout with the rice. Brush the trout with melted butter before baking. Bake about 20 minutes, until done. The fish will fall off the bone when done.

Bill Moriarty
Syracuse, New York

TROUT FILLETS A L'ORANGE

    2   trout fillets (5 oz. each)
    1   tsp. oil, margarine or butter
    1   shallot or 2 green onions, chopped
    4   mushrooms, sliced
        salt
        pepper
    2   tsp. grated fresh ginger, or 1 tsp. powdered ginger
  ½   cup orange juice
1½   T. lemon juice
    1   tsp. flour
    1   orange, sliced
    2   tsp. icing sugar
    2   sprigs fresh parsley, to garnish

Preheat the oven to 225°. Heat oil in a non-stick frying pan and brown the shallot and mushrooms. Move them to the side of the pan and add a few teaspoons of water. Place the trout in the pan, skin-side-up, and fry for a few minutes; flip and cook for a few minutes more, being careful not to overcook. Season the fillets to taste with salt and pepper, then remove them put them on 2 plates kept warm in the oven.

To make the sauce: In a small jar, combine the ginger, orange juice lemon juice and flour, then pour into the pan. Bring to a boil, then stir for 1-2 minutes, until thickened. Pour sauce over the fillets. Sprinkle the orange slices with sugar and heat briefly in the pan until caramelized.

Garnish the fillets with orange slices and parsley, and serve with steamed broccoli and couscous topped with snipped chives.

Leo G. J. Seffelaar
Broadview, Saskatchewan

CRAB-STUFFED TROUT

6	brook trout or salmon (8 oz. each), pan dressed
1/3	cup butter, divided
2	cups chopped fresh mushrooms
1/2	cup finely chopped onion
1/2	cup shredded carrot
1	cup flaked crabmeat (not imitation)
1/4	cup fine dry bread crumbs
2	T. chopped fresh parsley, divided
1½	tsp. white wine
1½	tsp. Worcestershire
2	tsp. lemon juice

To make the filling: In a 10 inch skillet over medium heat, cook the mushrooms, onion and carrot in 3 tablespoons hot butter until tender and the liquid has evaporated, stirring occasionally. In a medium bowl, combine the onion mixture, crabmeat, crumbs, 2 tablespoons parsley, the wine and Worcestershire sauce. Toss gently to coat. Spoon ½ cup of filling loosely into each fish cavity and secure with toothpicks.

To grill: Arrange the fish in an oiled grill basket. In a covered grill, arrange preheated coals around a drip pan. Place the grill basket on cooking grid over the pan. Cover and grill for 16-20 minutes, or until the fish begins to flake when tested, turning only once.

To broil: Arrange the fish on a rack in the broiler pan. Broil 6 inches from the heat for 16-20 minutes or until the fish begins to flake when tested, turning only once.

To make the sauce: In a 1-quart saucepan, combine the remaining butter, parsley and lemon juice. Heat over medium heat until the butter is melted, stirring occasionally. Serve the fish with the sauce.

Rod and Susanne Shafer
Salem, Oregon

TROUT PARMESAN AMANDINE

3-4 trout fillets (can substitute sole or orange roughy)
  1 T. of butter
3-4 T. sliced almonds
  3 large eggs
1½ T. Parmesan cheese
  1 T. chopped fresh parsley
    salt
    flour
    oil

Heat almonds in butter over low heat until slightly brown; set aside to cool. Beat the eggs in a bowl; mix in cheese and chopped parsley. Pat the fillets dry with a paper towel. Lightly salt the fillets and coat with flour. Heat the oil in a frying pan over medium. Dip each fillet in the egg mixture and then place in pan.

While fish is cooking, return almond butter to burner and warm on very low heat. Cook fillets for 2-3 minutes and turn over, cooking until they are opaque. Check with a fork on the thickest part of the fillet. (Be careful not to overcook. Fish will continue to cook for 2-3 minutes after being removed from heat.) Place fish on individual plates and top with almond butter to taste. Garnish with a sprig of parsley.

Recommended vegetable side dishes: cooked baby carrots in honey, creamed spinach, green and red bell pepper sauté, stir-fried green and yellow zucchini shoestrings.

Recommended starch side dishes: rice pilaf, fisherman's rice, boiled red potatoes.

Recommended wines: a dry white wine such as Johannisberg Riesling or Gray Riesling. For a sweeter, more fruity wine, try white Zinfandel.

Kevin Phillips
Santa Clara, California

SMOKED TROUT SPREAD

 1   cup of low-fat cottage cheese
1/2 lb. smoked trout or salmon
 3   oz. cream cheese, softened
 2   T. vodka
 1   heaping T. prepared horseradish
 1   T. fresh lemon juice
 2   tsp. coarse-grain mustard
 1   T. minced green onion
     pepper
     fresh dill sprigs or dried dill weed

Drain the excess liquid from the cottage cheese by placing it in a paper-towel-lined sieve. Press on the cheese and let it drain for 1/2 hour. Remove the skin and bones from the fish, then shred coarsely with a fork or fingertips. Place 2/3 of the fish in a food processor or blender. Add cottage cheese, cream cheese, vodka, horseradish, lemon juice and mustard. Process until smooth. Transfer the mixture to a bowl. Fold in the remaining fish and green onion. Season to taste with pepper. Chill.

To serve, spread on cocktail rye bread, crackers or crostini; garnish with dill.

Makes about 1¾ cups.

James S. Geddes
Cedarburg, Wisconsin

LAKE TROUT

lake trout fillets, cut   oil for frying
  into serving size   pepper
eggs, beaten   lemon
crackers, crushed

Dip the fillets in the eggs and then the cracker crumbs. Deep fry until golden, then season with pepper and lemon.

Steven Marcy
Ithaca, New York

TRUCHAS BORRACHAS "DRUNKEN TROUT"

4 trout, up to 14" long
1 can beer
1 cup yellow cornmeal
   salt
   pepper
4 T. oil

Soak trout in beer for 15 minutes, then dip in cornmeal. Salt and pepper to taste. Fry in oil in a frying pan until done.

Donald Ma
Albuquerque, New Mexico

SAUTÉED TROUT WITH ALMONDS

2 fresh trout fillets or butterflied trout,
     rainbow if possible
2 T. butter
½ cup slivered, toasted almonds
   flour
   salt
   pepper

Melt the butter in a large skillet and sauté the almonds until they just start to brown. Dredge the fillets in the flour and lay them, skin-side-up, on top of the almonds in the skillet. Salt and pepper to taste, and cook trout for about 5 minutes, or until lightly browned. Gently turn the fillets, making sure that the almonds stick to the fish, and sauté for another 5 minutes, or until browned and the fish flakes with a fork.

Seth Cowall
Harrisonburg, Virginia

Lake Trout Algonac

 1 lake trout (4 lbs.)
 1 tsp. salt
 1/4 tsp. pepper
 1/8 tsp. paprika

Dress trout, then wipe with a damp cloth. Blend the salt, pepper and paprika in a small dish. Rub the trout inside and out with this mixture. Bake at 350° for 1¼ hours, or until done.

Donn H. Jennins
Middletown, Ohio

Broiled Trout

 1 lb. trout fillets
 1 clove garlic, halved
 2 T. olive oil
 1/4 tsp. pepper
 4 T. butter, melted
 1 T. chopped parsley
 1 tsp. lemon juice

Rub a shallow bowl with the garlic and add the oil and pepper. Rub this mixture on both sides of the trout and place the fish on a broiling pan. Broil 4-5 inches from the heat, turning once, until the fish is golden brown and tender. Combine the butter, parsley and lemon juice and drizzle over the fish.

Optional: Bake fillets at 425°; allow 10 minutes per inch of thickness baking time.

Brian Taylor
New Cumberland, Pennsylvania

JOSH'S FRUITY TROUT MIX

1 10-12" trout fillet per person
1 can tropical fruit salad
2 T. iced tea mix
¼ cup blush Chablis
lemon juice, if desired

Place tropical fruit salad in a baking dish. Then add the trout fillets; mix. Add the tea mix. Mix some more. Bake in 400° oven for 3-5 minutes, adding wine after 3 minutes. Serve on a plate with lemon juice.

Larry Hooar
Granite Falls, North Carolina

TROUT PARMESAN

1-2 trout fillets (6-10 oz. each)
2 T. Parmesan cheese
⅓ tsp. sweet basil
butter or margarine

Mix the Parmesan and the sweet basil together in a bowl. Leave the fillets slightly wet and rub Parmesan mixture on the inside of the fillets (the wetness of the meat will help the coating adhere to the meat). Slip the fish into a medium-hot sauté pan with a little butter, margarine or other fat. Watch it closely so that it does not burn; it will take a minute or less to brown coating. Turn the fish over carefully, so as not to break the coating. Reduce heat and cook until done.

Works great on any fish. I premixed a container of this to take to Canada on a 185-mile canoe trip. It worked out great—no big prep mess.

Jeff Hendrickson
Cable, Wisconsin

GRILLED RAINBOW TROUT

1   lb. fresh trout fillets
    juice of ½ lemon
2   tsp. olive oil
    salt
    pepper
    paprika
1   clove garlic, minced
1   tsp. dried thyme leaves
1   lemon, cut into wedges

Prepare the coals. Arrange the trout fillets on a sheet of foil. Drizzle with lemon juice and olive oil. Sprinkle with salt, pepper, paprika, garlic and thyme. Grill over hot coals for about 8 minutes or until the fish flakes easily when pricked with a fork. Serve with fresh lemon.

Derek Spradlin
North Little Rock, Arkansas

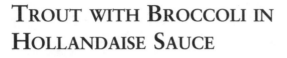

TROUT WITH BROCCOLI IN HOLLANDAISE SAUCE

4 14" fresh trout, filleted and skinned	ground ginger
1 cup lemon juice	ground allspice
1 ½ cups flour	1 lb. fresh broccoli
¾ cup butter, divided	2 packages hollandaise sauce mix
2 T. vegetable oil	1 lb. mushrooms, sliced
garlic powder	1 red onion, sliced
seasoned salt	2 whole lemons
pepper	parsley leaves

To prepare trout fillets, remove any bones with needle nose pliers. (Note: Run your hand against grain of the fillet to locate bones.) Rinse fillets. Pour lemon juice into a bowl, add the fillets and marinate for 1 hour.

Using a large plastic bag, add flour, then fillets, and shake thoroughly. Let them stand. Preheat a large skillet on medium-high. Add ½ cup of butter and the vegetable oil. Shake the fillets and lay them in the skillet. Lightly sprinkle the fillets with garlic powder, seasoned salt, pepper, ground ginger and ground allspice. Brown each side for 2-3 minutes, depending on thickness of the fillets. Do not overcook. Remove fillets from skillet and drain on paper towels.

Using a covered double boiler, steam the broccoli until it is tender, approximately 20 minutes. Using a saucepan, prepare the hollandaise sauce according to the directions on the package.

Using a large skillet, combine ¼ cup butter, mushrooms and onions; sprinkle with garlic powder and pepper. Cover and sauté for 7-10 minutes on medium heat, stirring occasionally.

Arrange 1-2 fillets on a serving plate with portions of broccoli covered with hollandaise sauce, mushrooms and onions. Garnish with lemon wedges and parsley leaves. Serve a fishing master's delight and enjoy.

Arnie Walk
Dugway, Utah

TROUT CUISINE

1 10-12" trout
    dry mustard powder
    garlic powder
    tartar seasoning
    meat tenderizer

Boil the trout for 10-15 minutes in a pan of water. Put foil on a cookie sheet and spray with non-stick cooking spray. Lay the trout on the foil and apply the mustard, garlic and tartar seasonings. Bake at 450° for 10-15 minutes. Apply the meat tenderizer and bake for 10-15 more minutes, or until the edges begin to brown. Then it is done.

Stephen Sechrist
Jersey Shore, Pennsylvania

TROUT IN BACON

6 or more small trout, cleaned and dried
12 or more bacon slices (2 for each fish)
    salt
    pepper

Wrap each trout in 2 pieces of bacon, holding them in place with toothpicks. Put the fish in a wire basket and grill them about 6 inches above the coals. When the bacon is crisp, the fish should be done. Salt and pepper to taste.

Dana Gould
Etna, Maine

BAKED STUFFED LAKE TROUT

1	8-10 lb. trout, cleaned and gilled
	salt
	pepper
	salad oil
½	cup butter or margarine, melted
¼	cup lemon juice

Vegetable stuffing:

1	cup onion, chopped
¼	cup butter or margarine
2	cups dry bread crumbs
1	cup coarsely shredded carrot
1	cup cut-up fresh mushrooms
½	cup snipped fresh parsley
1½	T. lemon juice
1	egg
2	tsp. salt
1	clove garlic, minced
¼	tsp. pepper

To make the stuffing: Cook and stir the onion in butter until the onion is tender. Lightly mix in the remaining stuffing ingredients.

Heat the oven to 350°. Wash the fish in cold water and pat dry. Rub the cavity with salt and pepper and stuff with the vegetable stuffing. Close the opening with skewers and lace with a string.

Brush the fish with salad oil and place it in an open shallow roasting pan. If possible, set the fish on a small grate to allow the fat to drip off. Bake for 1½ hours, or until the fish flakes easily. Baste with butter and lemon juice during the baking.

David Stokes
Duluth, Minnesota

FUSSY SCOTT'S FIRE TROUT

- 2-3 cleaned trout, any size
-   2 cups yellow cornmeal
-   2 T. cayenne pepper
-   1 tsp. chili powder
-   1 tsp. garlic powder
-   1 tsp. dried oregano
      peanut oil for frying

Combine all ingredients, except trout and oil, on a plate and mix thoroughly. Coat the trout in the mixture and fry in peanut oil until golden brown. This recipe works great with panfish as well.

Joseph J. Pipon III
Budd Lake, New Jersey

PAN-FRIED MACKINAW (LAKE TROUT) FILLETS

- 4-8 lake trout fillets
-   1 cup crushed cornflakes
-   1 cup crushed soda crackers
-   1 cup potato flakes
- 1-2 tsp. salt
-   1 tsp. pepper
-   1 T. margarine (or more, if necessary)
-   2 eggs, beaten
-   1 lemon, cut into wedges

Mix the cornflakes, crackers and potato flakes, salt and pepper. This mixture can be stored in a sealed container indefinitely. In a large frying pan, melt the margarine over medium-low heat. Pat the fillets dry, then dip into the eggs and roll in the crumbs until well coated. Fry as slow as you can so they will brown nicely, about 6-8 minutes per side, depending on the size of the fillets. Serve with the lemon wedges.

Evon L. Sizemore
Polson, Montana

RAINBOW TROUT WITH MUSHROOM STUFFING

    6   rainbow trout, cleaned and dried
    2   tsp. salt, divided
    4   cups soft bread cubes
  ²/₃   cup melted butter, divided
    1   cup sliced fresh mushrooms
  ³/₄   cup sliced green onions
  ¹/₄   cup chopped fresh parsley
    2   T. chopped pimentos
    4   tsp. lemon juice
  ¹/₂   tsp. dried marjoram

Salt the inside and outside of the fish with 1½ teaspoon of salt. Sauté the bread cubes in ½ cup melted butter until lightly browned. Add the mushrooms and onions, and cook until the mushrooms are tender. Add the remaining ½ tsp. salt, parsley, pimentos, lemon juice and marjoram, and toss lightly. Stuff the fish with bread crumb mixture and brush with the remainder of the butter. Bake in a greased dish for 25-30 minutes at 350°, or until the fish flakes.

Kenneth Turngren
New Castle, Delaware

BARBECUE RAINBOW TROUT

    1   whole trout (4 oz.-1 lb), cleaned with head,
          tail and skin intact
    2   tsp. butter or margarine
          garlic salt, to taste

Place the fish on a large sheet of aluminum foil, and put the butter or margarine inside the trout. Sprinkle on garlic salt, turn the trout over and sprinkle again. Cook over hot coals for 5-7 minutes per side.

Earl Scarborough
Rialto, California

TROUT FRIED IN OATMEAL

        1   lb. trout fillets, skinned
    1½   cups rolled oats
     ¼   cup milk
     ½   cup all-purpose flour
        2   eggs
    1½   tsp. salt
           freshly ground pepper
     ½   cup lard
           lemon wedges

Process the oats in a food processor until they are very fine, you should have about 1½ cups, and then spread them on a large plate. Pour the milk into a shallow bowl. Spread the flour on a separate large plate. Beat the eggs, salt, and freshly ground pepper to taste in a medium shallow bowl until well combined.

Working with 1 trout fillet at a time, dip the fillet in the milk, then in the flour, shaking off the excess. Then dip the fillet in the egg mixture, letting the excess drip back into the bowl. Finally, coat with the oats. Place the fish on a baking sheet, pressing the fillet with the flat side of a knife so the crumbs will adhere. Repeat this procedure with the remaining fillets. Place the baking sheet in the refrigerator for 20 minutes, or until ready to fry.

Heat the lard in a large skillet over medium-high heat until rippling. Fry the fillets in a single layer until the first sides are a golden brown, about 1½ minutes. Gently turn the fillets with a spatula; fry the other side until golden brown, about 1½ minutes. Transfer the fish to paper toweling to drain briefly. Keep them warm in an oven set to the lowest setting while you are frying the remaining fillets.

Serve immediately, garnished with lemon wedges.

Norma Blank
Shawano, Wisconsin

SMOKED TROUT IN TERIYAKI SAUCE

1	cleaned whole trout	1/8	tsp. salt
1	tsp. liquid smoke	1	tsp. brown sugar
1	T. teriyaki sauce	1/8	tsp. hickory smoked salt
1/8	tsp. red pepper	1/4	cup of margarine
1/8	tsp. black pepper		or butter

Clean the trout by removing the gills, the entrails and the blood vein along the backbone. Wash the fish thoroughly. Mix the liquid smoke and teriyaki sauce; brush in cavity of fish. Mix the spices and sprinkle over the fish. Rub a large piece of foil with margarine to keep the fish from sticking; wrap trout in foil. Place the trout in a smoker for 1 hour on medium to low heat. Use hickory or apple wood for smoking.

Doug Sander
Sarcoxie, Missouri

TUNA CASSEROLE

12	oz. fresh flaked tuna, or 2 cans of tuna, drained
1	12-14 oz. pkg wide noodles
1	can tomato soup
1	can Cheddar cheese soup
1/4	cup milk
1	T. fresh lemon juice
	salt
	pepper
1	cup grated sharp Cheddar cheese

Cook the noodles according to the package. Drain. Combine all of the ingredients, except for the noodles and grated cheese. Mix well; add noodles and toss. Put in a casserole and add a layer of cheese on the top. Bake at 350° for 45 minutes.

Mrs. Raymond D. Weikel
Hatboro, Pennsylvania

BALSAMIC TUNA

2	lbs. tuna cut into 2" pieces	¼	cup balsamic vinegar
1	cup flour, seasoned with salt/pepper	¼	cup water
		½	tsp. sugar
	olive oil for frying		salt
2	large onions, sliced		pepper

Wash and pat the tuna dry. Flour the tuna and fry in very hot olive oil until it is golden brown on both sides. Remove the tuna from the pan, and wipe the pan clean. Add more olive oil to the pan and add the onions. In a small bowl, mix the vinegar, water and sugar together; add to the pan with the onions, and cook over high heat until the mixture bubbles. Turn to low heat and season with salt and pepper. Return fish to the pan and continue cooking for 2 minutes, or until hot.

Anthony Maranzano
Staten Island, New York

BAKED WALLEYE FILLETS WITH SOUR CREAM AND CHEESE SAUCE

4-5	lbs. walleye fillets	1	cup sour cream
	lemon	⅔	cup grated Cheddar cheese
2	T. chopped onions	1	T. season salt

Place the fillets in a greased baking dish. Squeeze the lemon over the fish. Sprinkle the chopped onion over the fish. Cover with foil and bake at 350° for 20-30 minutes, or until the fish flakes easily with a fork. Mix together the sour cream, cheese and salt, and pour over the fish. Leave the foil off and place under the broiler for about 7 minutes, until brown and bubbly and heated through. Serve with lemon wedges, if desired.

Gordon Kremer
Sacramento, California

BROILED WALLEYE

fish fillets	pepper
lemon juice	Italian seasoning
melted margarine	parsley flakes
salt	paprika

Line the broiler pan with foil and fill the pan with the fillets; do not crowd them. Sprinkle with lemon juice and pour melted margarine over them. Sprinkle the rest of the ingredients over the fish and bake at 400° for 12-13 minutes, or until the fish is just flaky.

Have the rest of the meal ready, since the fish should be served immediately.

Jean and Martin Ode
San Benito, Texas

FISHERMAN'S FILLETS

6 large walleye fillets
  corn oil
1 cup crushed crackers
½ cup flour
½ tsp. salt
½ tsp. ground pepper
3 eggs, beaten
  lemon wedge or chives for garnish
  tartar sauce

Pat fillets dry with paper towels. Heat ⅛ inch of oil in a skillet over medium heat. Mix crackers, flour and salt in a bowl. Dip the fish into the eggs, then the crumbs. Pan-fry for 3 minutes, or until golden. Garnish and serve.

Joel Robinson
Grarb, North Dakota

SHRIMP AND WALLEYE CASSEROLE ON WILD RICE

3   lbs. walleye fillets, cut up into 1 x 2" pieces
2   cans cream of shrimp soup
1   can Parmesan cheese
1   box 5-minute wild rice mix
    Italian bread crumbs

Spoon some soup into the bottom of a 3-quart baking dish. Place a layer of cut-up walleye evenly on top. Sprinkle some Parmesan cheese over the fish. Repeat this until all of the fish is used. Sprinkle bread crumbs over top. Bake at 350° for 45-60 minutes, uncovered. Prepare wild rice according to package directions. Serve casserole on wild rice.

Robert L. Twichell
Fayetteville, New York

DEEP FRIED WALLEYE AND BISCUITS

    fresh walleye fillet   salt
    salt water   pepper
2   eggs   lard
1   box corn muffin mix   1   can ready-to-cook biscuits
    flour

Cut walleye into strips along the length of the fillet. Soak in salt water while preparing the batter. Beat eggs in a bowl. In a separate bowl, mix equal amounts of corn muffin mix and flour. Add salt and pepper to taste. Heat lard in deep-fryer it 375°.

Drain salt water off fillets, dip fillets into egg, then put fish in a large bread sack with flour mixture and shake. Drop fillets into hot grease and cook until they float to the top. Adjust cooking time to your taste — longer for crispy and shorter for a flaky texture.

After cooking fish, separate biscuits and cook in fish grease until brown. Fill with butter or jam for a quick dessert with shore lunch.

Larry Phillips
Marshal, Missouri

HONEY WALLEYE

4-6 walleye fillets (1½-2 lbs.)
  1 egg
  2 tsp. honey
  2 cups crushed butter-flavored crackers
  ½ tsp. salt
  ⅓ cup cooking oil
    lemon wedges

In a shallow bowl, beat egg and honey together. In a bag, combine the crackers and the salt. Dip the fish first in the egg mixture and then shake in the bag until coated. Fry in oil until golden brown, 3-5 minutes per side, until fish flakes easily with a fork. Serve with lemon wedges, if desired.

Gordon Kremer
Sacramento, California

POACHED ITALIAN WALLEYES

    walleye fillets
  2 pkgs. dry Italian dressing mix
  ½ cup white vinegar
  ½ cup water
  ¼ cup cooking oil
  5 T. lemon juice
  1 cup sour cream

Coat the fillets in dry Italian dressing mix. Mix the vinegar and water and stir well. Add the oil and lemon juice and stir again. Pour into a frying pan to ⅜ inch depth. Bring to a low boil and add the coated fillets. Poach until the meat flakes easily.

Wayne Anderson
Solon, Iowa

POTATO FLAKE WALLEYE

2   lbs. of walleye fillets (or any kind of
     fresh water fish)
2   eggs, beaten
1   cup milk
2   cups seasoned flour
     dry potato flakes
     oil for deep frying, heated to 350°

Mix the eggs and the milk well. Dredge the fish pieces in the flour, then dip then in the egg and milk mixture. Roll in the potato flakes. Deep fry in the hot oil until golden brown. Serve with creole tartar sauce (recipe below).

WALLEYE FISH BASKET

     walleye fillets (salmon and catfish are also good)
2   lbs. bacon
     red, green and yellow peppers, chopped
     onions, chopped
     mushrooms, sliced
     fish seasoning

Line the top and the bottom of a flat, square grilling basket with bacon. Lay the fish on top of the bacon and generously spread the vegetables and seasoning on. Repeat with another layer of fish. Close the basket and lay on the grill. The coals will flare up from the bacon grease. Cook for 20-30 minutes until the fish is done.

James Hoppe
Johnson Creek, Wisconsin

WALLEYE WITH MUSHROOM-CHEESE SAUCE

      6   walleye fillets, cut ½" thick (1½ lbs.)
   1½   cups sliced fresh mushrooms
      ½   cup sliced green onions
      ¼   tsp. pepper
      1   cup shredded Cheddar cheese
      1   can cream of mushroom soup
      1   cup sour cream

Pat the fish dry with a paper towel and arrange in a 12 x 8 x 2 inch baking dish. Top with the mushrooms, green onions and pepper. Sprinkle with cheese. Combine the mushroom soup and sour cream and carefully spoon mixture over the fish. Bake uncovered at 350° for 30 minutes, or until the fish flakes. Sprinkle additional green onions on top, if desired.

Gordon Kremer
Sacramento, California

WALLEYE FILLETS "MY WAY"

   4-6   small walleye fillets, cut into 3" pieces
      ⅓   cup Parmesan cheese
      3   T. biscuit mix
            butter or margarine

Mix the Parmesan and the biscuit mix in a paper bag. Add walleye and shake to coat. In a skillet or electric frying pan, cook fillets in the hot butter or margarine until golden brown on both sides and the fillets flake easily with a fork.

Gordon Kremer
Sacramento, California

CRISPY WALLEYE WITH CHILI SAUCE

6   nice walleye fillets
1   egg, beaten
2   T. milk
1   tsp. salt
1   tsp. chili powder
5-6   drops of hot
        pepper sauce
½   cup yellow
        cornmeal
½   cup flour
        oil for frying
1   bottle chili
        sauce

Dick Giluk

Clean, wash and dry the fish. Combine the egg, milk, salt, chili powder and hot pepper sauce.

Combine the cornmeal and flour. Dip the fish in the egg mixture, then roll in the cornmeal mixture. Fry in oil at moderate heat for about 5 minutes; turn, and fry for 5 more minutes, until the fish are brown and flake easily. Pat dry with a paper towel and cover with chili sauce.

Dick Giluk
Jackson, Michigan

EARL'S FOILED WALLEYE

2-3   lbs. fresh walleye fillets (any freshwater fish)
2   tsp. lemon juice
   black pepper, Cajun spice, oregano, garlic powder
1   onion, sliced in rings
1   green pepper, sliced in rings
1   tomato, sliced in rings
   salt
1   T. butter
1½   tsp. olive oil

Wash fillets in cold water and place on individual sheets of foil. Sprinkle on lemon juice, then add spices to taste. Garnish with rings of onion, pepper and tomato. Top with butter and oil. Wrap foil over fillets and double-fold for a secure seal. Grill or bake on medium heat for 15 minutes. Flip, then continue cooking an additional 15 minutes. Check fillets for doneness. If needed, grill or bake an additional 15 minutes per side.

Note: Make additional servings (minus the tin foil, oil, butter, and spices), and freeze in individual freezer bags. Frozen fish will thaw quickly if you run bag under cold water. Add butter, oil, spices, wrap in foil and grill. Makes an excellent snack when the craving hits.

Robert "Earl" Shafer
Roseville, Minnesota

GRILLED WALLEYE

    walleye fillet (or any other fillet that is 1/2 to
      1" thick)
2/3 cup soy sauce
1/2 cup ketchup
2 T. lemon juice
2 T. vegetable oil
1 tsp. crushed dried rosemary

Place the walleye in a single layer in a plastic bag or glass baking dish. Combine the soy sauce, ketchup, lemon juice, oil and rosemary, and pour into bag or dish. Cover or close bag and let stand for 1 hour, turning once. Remove the fillets, reserving the marinade. Place the fillets in a well-greased hinged wire basket.

Grill, covered, over medium coals for 8-10 minutes, or until the fish is browned on the bottom. Turn and baste with marinade; grill 5-7 minutes longer or until the fish flakes easily with a fork.

For a better smoke flavor, use a wood fire or wood chips on your grill.

J. Frank Jackson
Newark, Ohio

SPICY BARBECUE WALLEYE

    2 or more walleye fillets   hot sauce to taste
1 large onion, chopped   (not more than 6 drops)
1 green pepper, chopped   garlic salt to taste
    red pepper to taste   1 bottle barbecue sauce

Mix all the ingredients, except the fillets and the barbecue sauce, together. Make an aluminum foil tray with 1 inch deep sides and place it on the grill, keeping the grill on low. Cover the bottom of tray with at least 1/4 inch of barbecue sauce. Place the walleye fillets in the tray and cover with the mixed ingredients. Grill on low for 15-25 minutes, turning the fillets over periodically.

Jason Lucas
Saline, Michigan

GRILLED WALLEYE FILLETS WITH LEMON PEPPER

2 walleye fillets
½ T. lemon pepper
¼ cup diced onion
2 T. butter
  aluminum foil

Place the walleye fillets on a sheet of aluminum foil approximately 2 feet in length. Sprinkle the lemon pepper and onion over the fillets. Place half the butter at each end of the fillets. Seal all of the contents inside the foil. Place package on a preheated grill for approximately 15 minutes, flipping the package halfway through the cooking time. The cooking time may vary depending on the thickness of the fillets. They walleye is cooked when it is tender and flaky to the touch of a fork.

Steve Crew
Clive, Iowa

WALLEYE AT ITS BEST

6 fresh walleye fillets
2 T. olive oil
2 T. sweet cream butter (not margarine)
3 large eggs, beaten
10 crackers, crushed finely
  salt
  pepper

Heat the olive oil and butter in a frying pan on medium to medium-high heat until the butter is golden. Take the fresh fillets and dip them in the beaten egg. Lift each fillet for a second to let the excess egg drain off. Then dip the fish in the crushed crackers. Fry to a flaky golden brown. Salt and pepper to taste.

Other fish also work well. Be an adventurer, try some celery salt with your seasonings.

Vernon F. Davis
Milnor, North Dakota

DEEP-SOUTH WALLEYE AND OYSTER FRY

1¹/₂ lbs. walleye, perch or bass fillets
12   oysters, shucked, or 1 jar medium oysters, drained
1   cup all-purpose flour
     pinch cayenne pepper
     salt
     pepper
¹/₂ cup milk
     dash of hot pepper sauce
1   cup fine yellow cornmeal
     vegetable oil for frying

Combine the flour, cayenne, salt and pepper to taste on a plate and stir to mix. In a shallow bowl, combine the milk with a dash (or more) of hot sauce. Put the cornmeal in a third shallow dish.

Cut each fish fillet into 2-4 equal pieces, depending on their size. Dry the fish and oysters well on paper towels. Heat about 2 inches of oil to 375° in a deep fryer. Dust the fish pieces with the seasoned flour, shaking off the excess. Dip them in the milk, allow the excess to drip off, and then thoroughly coat them in the cornmeal. Shake off the excess cornmeal, and add the fish to the hot oil. Fry, turning once or twice, until golden and crisp, 5-7 minutes. Drain on paper towels and keep warm in the oven until ready to serve. Repeat with the oysters, frying them 2-3 minutes.

Leo G. J. Seffelaar
Broadview, Saskatchewan

HEALTHY WALLEYE

walleye fillets
salsa
low-fat shredded
cheese

Put the walleye fillets in tin foil and cover them with your favorite salsa. Close up the foil and cook until just done. Open the foil and cover the fish with the shredded cheese. Put it back over the heat, uncovered, until the cheese melts.

Bob Keeney

This fish may be cooked in the oven or over the barbecue. Makes an easy shore lunch, too.

Bob Keeney
Brighton, Michigan

WALLEYE LASAGNA

       white fish fillets (walleye, perch, bass)
$1/2$ onion, finely cut
 1   leek, finely cut
$1/2$ cup sliced mushrooms
       butter
$1/2$ cup white wine
 4   cups fish broth
 1   T. chopped garlic
 1   T. chopped fresh chervil
       pinch salt
       pinch pepper
 1   branch tarragon
       pinch dried thyme
 1   bay leaf
 1   cup heavy cream
$1/3$ cup cornstarch
       lasagna noodles
       mozzarella or Gruyère cheese

To make the lasagna sauce: Sauté the onion, leek, and mushrooms in butter until tender. Add the wine, fish broth, and all of the seasonings. Cook very slowly, adding the cream and cornstarch. Taste and season, if necessary.

Cook the lasagna noodles, per package directions. In a large lasagna pan, put a layer of noodles, then the fish fillets, some sauce and cheese. Repeat this step 3 times. Cook in a 400° oven until the cheese is crunchy.

Paul A. Garceau
Meriden, Connecticut

CEVICHE KEBABS

1   lb. white fish fillets (walleye, sole, perch, haddock)
1   T. olive oil
2   T. lemon juice
1   T. lime juice
3   T. orange juice
3   T. chopped fresh cilantro
    salt
    pepper
3   oranges
1   T. Dijon mustard
1   cucumber, peeled, seeded and diced
    avocados, ripe but slightly firm, peeled and diced

Slice the fish into strips, then into ½ inch cubes. In a shallow bowl, whisk together the olive oil, lemon, lime and orange juices, half of the cilantro, and salt and pepper to taste. Add the fish to the marinade and toss gently until well coated. Cover and refrigerate for 5-8 hours, stirring occasionally.

Peel the oranges, taking care to remove all of the white. Halve the oranges crosswise and remove each section from its skin with a small knife.

Add the remaining cilantro, Dijon mustard, cucumber, and avocado to oranges; toss gently until well coated.

On long toothpicks, spear a piece of avocado, an orange section, a cube of fish, a piece of cucumber, and another cube of fish. To serve, stick the toothpicks into several oranges.

Scallops can be used instead of white fish.

Leo G. J. Seffelaar
Broadview, Saskatchewan

BATTERS AND SAUCES

CINDY LOU MALANDER'S BEER BATTER

       fish fillets of your choice
1   can of beer
4   eggs, beaten
       bread crumbs
½   cup vegetable oil
       salt
       lemon pepper

Soak the fish for 1 hour in the beer, then rinse. Dip the fish in the eggs and then the bread crumbs. Heat oil in a large skillet and fry the fish until each side is browned. When the fish is almost done, add a little water, turn down the heat, and steam until cooked through. Season with salt and lemon pepper.

Cindy Louise Malander
Pillager, Minnesota

CRUNCHY CORNMEAL FISH

1   cup flour
¼   cup yellow cornmeal
1   tsp. lemon pepper
1   can beer
2   eggs
       oil for frying

Mix dry ingredients in 1 bowl; eggs and beer in another. Dip fish into beer and egg batter, then roll in flour mixture. Deep fry in oil until golden brown.

Fred Schmidtke
Sullivan, Missouri

TARTAR SAUCE

- ⅛ cup mayonnaise
- 3 T. pickle or tomato relish
- 2 tsp. minced(instant) onion
- 1 T. lemon juice
- ¼ tsp. dry mustard
- ¼ tsp. celery salt

Combine all ingredients and mix well. Refrigerate for 1 hour, allowing flavors to blend. Serve with baked, broiled or fried fish and seafood, or salmon croquettes. Makes 1 cup.

Lewis Drullinger and Jody Brown
Woodstock, Kansas

BREADED FISH

-   fish
- 2 cups flour
- 2 cups crushed cornflakes
- 2 tsp. garlic salt
- 2 tsp. paprika
- 4 tsp. salt
- 1 tsp. pepper
-   oil for frying

Combine all ingredients, except fish and oil; roll fish in mix. Fry fish in oil in pan until done.

Jeffrey P. Jensen
Tremonton, Utah

BEER BATTER FOR YOUR FAVORITE CATCH

1-2   lbs. fish fillets (bluegill, crappie, walleye, bass, or your favorite)
   2   cups flour
   1   12-oz bottle or can of your favorite beer
   1   tsp. paprika
   1   tsp. dried dill weed
   1   tsp. dried chives
   1   tsp. parsley flakes
   1   tsp. garlic powder
  ½   tsp. lemon zest
  ½   tsp. orange zest
       pepper
       salt (optional)
       oil for frying

Rinse fillets. Mix flour and beer; if the batter is too thick, use more beer to make it thinner; for a thicker batter, use less beer. Then add the rest of the ingredients to the batter. Dip the fillets in the batter, and deep fry or fry in a pan in 375° oil until golden brown. Then bake the fillets for about 20-30 minutes at 350° or until fish just flake apart.

Andrew S. Dzuracky
Lowellville, Ohio

TARTAR SAUCE

   1   cup mayonnaise
  ¼   cup pickle relish
       squeeze of lemon juice
   1   tsp. garlic

Mix well and adjust to taste.

Aaron Galindo
San Antonio, Texas

COTTAGE CHEESE AND SHRIMP DIP

1 8-oz. can premium select shrimp, chopped
1 16-oz. container low-fat cottage cheese
3-4 green onions, finely chopped

Combine the shrimp (including a little juice from the can) with the cottage cheese and the onions. Mix well and chill.

Serve with potato chips.

Daniel Wilson
Crockett, California

JIM'S FISH BREADING

fish
1 cup pancake mix
$1/4$ cup flour
$1/8$ tsp. baking powder
1 tsp. paprika
1 can of lemon-lime soda
1-2 dashes of hot pepper sauce
oil for frying

Mix the dry ingredients together; combine soda and pepper sauce in separate dish. Dip fish first in the dry ingredients and then in the soda. Fry in 350° oil until done.

Jim Davis
Kokomo, Indiana

SMOKED SALMON DIP

    1   salmon
        table salt
    1   can beer
        tomato juice
    2   T. mayonnaise
    1   T. yellow mustard

Step 1: Catch, or have someone give you, a salmon.

Step 2: Remove the innards, all fins, the tail and the head.

Step 3: With the skin and scales intact, cut the fish, cross-grain, into pieces approximately 2-2½ inches thick.

Step 4: Using a stock pot, or similar deep pot, place the fish pieces in layers so that most of the surface of the fish is exposed. Cover the fish with a water and salt brine (you need enough salt to allow a raw egg to float in the brine). Let this sit for 8 hours (no salt taste), 10 hours (slight salt taste), or 12 hours (somewhat salty taste).

Step 5: Dump the slimy salt brine and rinse the fish under cold running water to remove the excess slime/salt.

Step 6: Place the cleaned salmon pieces in a smoker for 2½-2¾ hours from the time you light the match. This time depends on the outside temperature, the wind, etc. I use a smoker with a charcoal pan (filled with charcoal and 4-5 chunks of water-soaked wood chips — hickory if available), a filled water pan with 1 can beer added to it, and 2 grills. I can process 2-17 pounds of salmon at the same time using both grills.

Step 7: Remove the salmon after the meat has dropped down the backbone approximately ½ inch or so. Let it cool for an hour or until you can handle it without burning your fingers.

Step 8: Remove the bones from the salmon. Place the smoked salmon pieces into pint canning jars. Fill each jar with tomato juice, leaving ½ inch head space.

Step 9: Process jars in a pressure cooker at 10 pounds for 100 minutes.

Step 10: To make the final product, drain, but save, the tomato juice from fish. Set the juice aside for now. Mix in the mayonnaise and the mustard. Stir until well mixed and somewhat creamy. If it is not creamy enough, add a small amount of the tomato juice you have saved.

Serve with sesame or similar crackers. I'd suggest you not set this on the table until you have had your fill because it won't last long. What with a week's vacation, lures, line, license, slip rental, food, liquid refreshments, etc., the first pint cost me about $400. All the rest were free.

Vernon A. Denzer
Dane, Wisconsin

CREOLE TARTAR SAUCE

- 2 cups mayonnaise
- 1 bunch green onions, chopped
- 1 red pepper, diced
- 3 T. Cajun seasoning

Mix all ingredients well. Tartar sauce will keep in the refrigerator for about 4 weeks.

Arnold Dunn
Cottage Grove, Minnesota

ZAMBIA FISH BATTER

1   lb. fish, cut up
    oil for frying
2   T. flour
½   tsp. salt
½   tsp. baking soda
1   T. white vinegar
2   T. water

Heat 3 inches of oil in a deep, heavy pan to 375°. Wash and dry the fish. Mix the flour and the salt together in 1 bowl and the baking soda and vinegar together in another bowl. Then add the vinegar mixture to the flour mixture and stir well. Add the water and beat until smooth. If the batter is too thick, add more water. Let the batter rest for 10 minutes.

Dip the fish into the batter and fry in oil until golden brown.

William S. Richards
Silver Bay, Minnesota

SEAFOOD TACO DIP

8   oz. cream cheese, softened
½   cup sour cream
¼   cup mayonnaise
10 oz. imitation crab, chopped
½   cup shredded mozzarella cheese
1   chopped green pepper
1   chopped red pepper
3   diced green onions
1   chopped tomato

Whip together the cream cheese, sour cream, and mayonnaise; spread on a large pizza pan. Layer the rest of the ingredients on top and serve with tacos or tortilla chips.

Leo G. J. Seffelaar
Broadview, Saskatchewan

SOUPS AND CHOWDERS

HAROLD GARRETT'S FISH CHOWDER

	chunks of fish (bluegill, crappie, bass, walleye, etc.)
4	large potatoes, peeled and diced
2	large onions, diced
4	stalk of celery, diced
1	can corn
1	can peas
1	can cream of mushroom soup
1/2	cup margarine
1/2	cup flour or pancake mix
1	can evaporated milk

Cover the potatoes, onions and celery with water in soup pot and cook until tender. Drain and save the water. Add the rest of the ingredients, except flour and milk, and cook until the fish is tender. Add flour and enough of the saved water to make the chowder fluid, but not runny. Add the evaporated milk and heat through.

Harold Garrett
Normal, Illinois

TROUT CHOWDER

2	trout	1	can evaporated milk
3	potatoes	1	T. butter
1/2	can corn		salt
1	onion (optional)		pepper

Pare and dice the potatoes and place in a pan. Cover them with water and slowly cook until they are about half done. Place the trout in a separate pan, cover with water, and boil for about 5 minutes to remove the meat from the bones. Remove the bones from the water and add the corn, onion, milk, potatoes, butter, salt and pepper to taste. Cook slowly until desired thickness is achieved, about 10 minutes and serve.

Scott Green
Salt Lake City, Utah

FISH SOUP

8   oz. fresh or frozen fish fillets, cut in 1" pieces
2   cups water
1   can tomatoes, cut up with the liquid
2   cups frozen mixed vegetables
1   cup thinly sliced celery
3/4 cup chopped onion
1¹/₂ tsp. instant chicken bouillon granules
1   tsp. dried oregano, crushed
1   clove garlic, minced
    several dashes bottled hot pepper sauce

In a large saucepan, combine all of the ingredients except the fish. Bring to a boil, reduce heat, cover, and simmer for 10 minutes or until the vegetables are tender. Stir in fish, return to a boil, then reduce the heat. Cover and simmer gently for about 5 minutes, or until the fish flakes easily with a fork.

Tim Ferrell
Conway, South Carolina

FISH CHOWDER

 2 cups diced raw boneless fish
 6 cups water
1½ tsp. salt
 1 cup diced celery
 1 cup diced onion
 2 cups diced potatoes
 3 strips bacon, crisp fried and crushed
 1 can mushroom soup
 1 can evaporated milk
 2 tsp. hot pepper sauce

Bring the salted water to a boil. Add celery and cook for 3 minutes. Add onion, potatoes and bacon; cook until potatoes are tender. Add fish and cook for 2 minutes, then add mushroom soup and milk. Add hot sauce, simmer 8 minutes, and then serve.

Dale Byren
South Haven, Minnesota

DICK'S MUSSEL AND CORN CHOWDER

2	lbs. mussels
1/4	lb. salt pork
4-5	ears of corn
1	large onion
	garlic to taste
2	medium potatoes
2	cups half-and-half (or a little more)
1	cup sour cream (optional)
	fresh nutmeg

Steam the mussels until they open, reserving the stock. Remove the mussels from their shells and chop coarsely. Remove and discard the rind from the pork. Cut the pork into 1/4 inch cubes. In a small stock pot, cook the salt pork until crisp (called cracklings). Set aside the cracklings with about 2 tablespoon of fat. Cut the kernels off the ears of corn with a sharp knife, then milk the ears into a bowl. Cut the onion in half and slice thinly.

In the stock pot, sauté the onion and garlic in the reserved fat. Cut the potatoes into small cubes and add to the pot along with the corn and the reserved mussel stock (about 6 cups). Simmer for 10 minutes. Add the half-and-half and simmer until the potatoes are tender. Remove from the heat and add the sour cream and blend with a whisk. Return to the heat and add the mussels. Heat but do not boil. Serve immediately, sprinkled with the freshly grated nutmeg.

For a thicker chowder, purée about half the corn.

Richard LeClair
Leicester, Massachusetts

ST. LAWRENCE RIVER GUIDE'S FISH CHOWDER

2 lbs. northern pike fillets, cubed
2 quarts water
2 lbs. northern pike fillets, cubed
4 large onions, diced
1 bunch celery, sliced
1 pound carrots, sliced
4 large cans whole tomatoes
2 large cans tomato sauce
1 lb. slab bacon or salt pork, cubed
5 lbs. potatoes, cubed
   salt
   pepper

In large pot, combine water, onions, celery, carrots, tomatoes and tomato sauce. Bring to a boil, reduce heat cover, and simmer. In a skillet, brown bacon or salt pork. Drain grease and add bacon to pot. (I prefer bacon for its smoked flavor). Slowly stir in cubed pike fillets. Continue simmering for 4 hours. Add potatoes, salt and pepper to taste, cover, and simmer for one more hour, or until potatoes are cooked.

Optional: If you prefer more fish flavor, boil fish bones in a cheesecloth bag in the 2 quarts water before cooking other ingredients, then discard the bones.

Dale L. Houghton
St. Lawrence River, New York

HAROLD'S FISH STEW

Get your rod, reel, and fish stuff together and go catch a big "un." Probably won't cost more than fifty dollars and a half a day; or go to the market and buy about 6-7 pounds of fish for above 12 dollars, 5 pounds of potatoes, and 4 pounds of onions. Boil the fish until the meat will slip from the bone (boil in salty water).

Cut your potatoes in cubes about as large as the fingernail on your left thumb. Cut the onions about the same size. Then choose a 3-gallon pot and place about 2-3 tablespoons of olive oil in the bottom of the pot. Layer the pot with the cubes of potatoes, then a layer of onion, and then a layer of fish. Now, at this point you need to season the contents of the pot with salt and black pepper. Also, I like to add a generous portion of Cajun seasonings to this stew. Then continue to layer the potatoes and onions and fish and season again until all of the ingredients are in the pot.

Then pour tomato sauce over the ingredients, until it is all covered, don't be sparing with the tomato sauce. (Do not use any water in this, there will be enough as it is.)

Start off cooking very slow on low heat until stew gets warm; increase the heat to about medium. Don't hurry this stew, just a slow simmer is all you need. Continue to cook this way until the potatoes and onions are cooked done and the seasoning has worked into the stew. Then it's serving time!

Never, never stir this pot with a spoon or any other utensil. Stir the pot by twisting it around back and forth. Serve as hot as you can stand to eat it and don't get hurt in the traffic going back for more.

Harold Bush
North Augusta, South Carolina

OLD-FASHIONED CATFISH SOUP

1½ lbs. catfish fillets, washed and cubed
  1 medium onion, sliced thin
  2 cloves garlic, finely minced
  2 T. butter or margarine
  6 qts. water
 ¾ cup tomato juice or tomato-vegetable juice blend
       (more if desired)
  4 ears of fresh sweet corn, cooked and corn cut
       from the cob
  4 ribs celery, diagonally cut into ½" slices
  3 fresh medium tomatoes, peeled, seeded
       and chopped
  3 medium potatoes, diced into 1" cubes
  1 lb. fresh green beans, diagonally cut into
       1½" pieces
 ½ cup chopped fresh parsley
  3 medium carrots, diagonally cut into ½" slices
  1 cup fresh peas
  1 cup fresh lima beans
     salt
     pepper

In an 8-quart kettle, sauté the onion and garlic in the butter until the onions are wilted. Add the water and the tomato juice. Add the cubed catfish and lightly boil for 5 minutes. Add the remaining ingredients, and cook to the desired tenderness. Simmer for 1 hour (less if you want crisp-tender vegetables). Adjust the seasoning to individual taste, and add more water, if needed.

Patricia Snider
Marblehead, Ohio

176

CHEEK MEAT CHOWDER

cheek and head meat from 2 striped bass
  (3-4 lbs. meat)
water
2 bay leaves
5 cups cubed potatoes
1/2 cup butter
2 large onions, minced
2 cloves garlic,
    minced
1/4 cup flour
4 cups milk
1 cup cream
2 cups half-and
    -half
2 tsp. salt
1/2 tsp. pepper

Tom McConnell

In a large kettle, cover the fish heads with water, add the bay leaves, and bring to a boil. Cook until the meat flakes off the heads. Place the meat in a bowl and set aside. Remove the bay leaves. Save 4 cups of fish stock from the kettle. Add the potatoes to the stock and cook on medium heat until the potatoes are tender.

While the potatoes are cooking, melt the butter in a saucepan.

Add the onions and garlic and sauté until the onions are tender. Stir in the flour and cook for two minutes. Add the mixture to the kettle containing the cooked potatoes. Stir in the fish meat. Add the milk, cream, half-and-half, salt and pepper. Heat, but do not boil.

Tom McConnell
Albuquerque, New Mexico

PANFISH CHOWDER

1½ cups cut-up cooked panfish (about 1½" pieces)
6 slices bacon, cut up
3 medium red potatoes (about 1 lb.)
⅔ cup chopped onion
½ cup chopped celery
2 cups fish stock (or substitute 2 cups water and
    2 tsp. instant chicken bouillon granules, and omit
    the 1 tsp. salt)
1 cup sliced fresh mushrooms
½ cup chopped carrot
¼ cup snipped fresh parsley
1 T. fresh lemon or lime juice
1 tsp. salt
½ tsp. dried dill weed
⅛ tsp. dried fennel seed
⅛ tsp. garlic salt
⅛ tsp. pepper
1 cup half and half

In a 3 quart saucepan, cook the bacon over medium-high heat, stirring occasionally, until crisp. Remove with a slotted spoon and set aside. Peel the potatoes and cut into ¾ inch cubes and set aside.

Cook and stir the onion and celery in the bacon fat over medium-high heat until tender, about 5 minutes. Add the bacon, potato cubes, fish stock, mushrooms, carrot, parsley, lemon juice, salt, dill weed, fennel, garlic salt, and pepper. Heat to boiling, reduce the heat and cover and simmer until the vegetables are tender, 15-20 minutes. Blend in the half and half. Gently stir in the fish pieces. Skim the fat, if desired.

David Patrick Valverde
Searcy, Arizona

CIOPPINO (FISH STEW)

2 lbs. fish fillets (cod, haddock, etc.)
2 medium onions, chopped
2 garlic cloves, chopped
2 T. olive or vegetable oil
1 large can of tomatoes
1 T. mixed pickling spices
½ tsp. salt
   a few grains of pepper

Cut the fillets into pieces about 2 inches square. In a deep saucepan,
fry the onions and garlic in oil until soft and golden colored. Add the
tomatoes, the pickling spice (tied in a cheesecloth bag), salt and pepper.
Simmer for 20 minutes. Remove the spice bag and bring the liquid to the
to a boil. Add the fish pieces and simmer gently for about 7 minutes,
until the fish flakes easily when tested with a fork.
Serve immediately

Leo G. J. Seffelaar
Broadview, Saskatchewan

Shrimp and Fish Chowder

1½   lbs. chunked fillet panfish or walleyes
¼   lb. shrimp
2-3   cups water
3   medium potatoes, diced
½   lb. bacon, fried and crumbled
½   tsp. salt
¼   tsp. pepper
2   medium onions, chopped
1   tsp. flour
1   pint half and half
    milk
1   T. butter

In a saucepan, bring the water to a boil. Add the potatoes and cook until they are ¾ done. Add the fish, shrimp, bacon, salt, pepper, and onions. Cook until the potatoes are done.

Add the flour to the half-and-half. Add the milk until chowder is desired consistency and stir well. Add the butter, stirring until the butter is melted.

Wayne Anderson
Solon, Iowa

Bluegill Stew and French Fried Fish Tails

2   dozen bluegill fillets   salt
    fish tails   pepper
2   duck eggs   oil for frying
6   cans of beer

Start with a pot. Pour in 1 cup of water and salt and pepper. Bring to a simmer. Add bluegill fillets, duck eggs, beer.

Fire up a deep fryer and drop the fish tails in one at a time, not in a bundle.

Dan Parker
Delaware, Ohio

PERCH CHOWDER

20	medium to large perch fillets, diced
1	onion, diced
2	green peppers, diced
1/2	butter
4	medium potatoes
1-2	cups corn
6	strips of bacon or ham
2	cups of milk
1	jar diced pimientos
2	tsp. chicken bouillon granules
	salt
	white pepper

Boil the diced perch in enough water to just cover the top of them, until tender. Sauté the onion and green pepper in butter. Boil the potatoes for about 10 minutes, drain and peel if desired. Cut them into chunks. Add the potatoes, onion, green pepper, corn, soup, milk, pimientos, chicken bouillon, salt and pepper to the perch in the water. Dice and fry the bacon until it is crisp. Add to the soup. Simmer (do not boil) for 30-45 minutes.

Serve with oyster crackers or salty crackers.

Ben Crooke
Mandan, North Dakota

CARP STEW

4 lbs. carp
1/4 lb. bacon
1/4 cup chopped onion
1 cup chopped tomatoes
1/4 tsp. salt
1/2 tsp. sugar

Fry the bacon in a Dutch oven or small kettle until crisp. Add the remaining ingredients and simmer for 45 minutes.

Michael Burgess
Rolla, Missouri

TROUT CHOWDER

1 trout
6-7 cups of water
5 potatoes, diced
1 cup diced celery
1 cup diced onion
2 cans evaporated milk
1 can cream of mushroom soup
1 can precooked shrimp
salt
garlic salt
pepper
parsley

Microwave the trout on high for 7 minutes, covered. Debone the trout. Bring the water to a boil in a large pot with the potatoes, celery, onion and fish. Boil until these ingredients are tender, and then add the milk, soup and shrimp. Season to taste with the salts, pepper and parsley. Heat through, stirring often.

Larry Schwartz
Dolores, Colorado

KALA MOJAKKA (FINNISH FISH SOUP)

2 lbs. fish fillets
1 tsp. salt
6 large potatoes, peeled and cut up small
½ cup diced celery
½ cup diced carrots
½ cup diced onion
¼ cup peppercorns
1 qt. whole milk
½ stick of butter

Place the salt and the fish into 1 quart of water and boil until the fish flakes or until the bones can be picked out. If there are bones, pick them out. In a separate large kettle, boil the potatoes, celery, carrots, onion, and peppercorns (with just enough water to cover them) until the potatoes are tender. Add vegetables to the fish and the water it was boiled in; add milk and butter. Bring to a simmer and simmer for 10 minutes. Serve hot; salt and pepper to taste.

Note: Old-timers often used the fish heads and tails and eliminated the celery and carrots.

Aro Saari
Nashwauk, Minnesota

SEAMAN'S HOTWATER CORNCAKES
(TO BE SERVED WITH FISH)

2 cups yellow cornmeal
1 tsp. salt

a pot of boiling water
oil for frying

Put the cornmeal into a mixing bowl and add the salt, stirring very well. Have the pot of boiling water ready. At the same time, heat a frying pan with about ¼ inch of oil. Mix the hot water with the cornmeal and stir well. Put the cornmeal mix into the frying pan a tablespoonful at a time. Brown on both sides.

You can adjust the salt to taste. The key, though, is to make sure the hot water is boiling when you mix it up. You must have everything ready, which is not hard for a good camper.

John A. Seaman
Ooltewah, Tennessee

HUSH PUPPIES

1 cup self-rising cornmeal mix (yellow is preferable)
¼ cup self-rising flour
½ tsp. fresh ground black pepper
½ tsp. salt (optional)
1 egg
¼ cup milk
½ medium onion, finely minced
  zest from 1 large lemon, finely minced
2 T. jalapeño pepper rings, chopped, or 2 fresh
  jalapeño peppers, seeded and chopped
  peanut oil for frying, heated to 350°

Mix together dry ingredients in a bowl, blending well. Beat the egg and add milk to it, then add that mixture to the dry ingredients. Add onion, lemon zest and peppers; mix. If batter is too thick, add more milk. Drop by teaspoons into hot peanut oil and fry until golden brown. For an additional treat, serve hush puppies with guava jelly.

Charles E. Chastain
Memphis, Tennessee

YOUR FAVORITE FISH RECIPE

Seafood Stick Vol-au-Vent

12	seafood sticks, diced
2	T. butter
1/2	onion, finely chopped
1/2	carrot, chopped
1/4	celery stalk, chopped
2	T. curry powder
3	T. flour
1 1/2	cups chicken stock, heated
	salt
	pepper
1/4	cup heavy cream
1	tsp. chopped parsley
1/2	cup canned mandarin oranges, drained
4	vol-au-vent shells(puff pastry shells), baked

Heat the butter in a frying pan. When hot, add the onion, carrot and celery. Cover and cook for 3-4 minutes over medium heat. Mix in the curry powder and flour. Cook 1 minute, uncovered, over medium heat. Pour in the chicken stock and season well with salt and pepper.

Cook for 8-10 minutes, uncovered, over medium heat. Add the cream and the parsley and mix well. Continue cooking for 3-4 minutes. Stir in the seafood sticks and the mandarins and simmer for 2-3 minutes over low heat. Fill the vol-au-vent shells and serve.

Leo G. J. Seffelaar
Broadview, Saskatchewan

JOE SILER'S STIR-FRIED FISH

2½ cups 1 x 1 x ½" cubed fish (no bones)
1 cup white rice (not minute rice)
1 can chicken broth
1½ cups water
¼ cup chopped onion
¼ cup lemon juice
garlic salt

Combine the rice, chicken broth, water and onion, and cook until done. Soak the fish in lemon juice for 30 minutes. Cook the fish in a wok that has been sprayed with cooking spray until done, then add the rice. Cook an additional 6-7 minutes, then add garlic salt to taste.

Joe Siler
Harleton, Texas

Joe Siler

SUMMER FRIED FISH

1	lb. fish fillets or 3-4 lbs. fresh, cleaned fish
1	egg, beaten
1/4	cup milk
1/2	cup ground oat flour*
2	tsp. dry mustard
1	tsp. baking powder
1	tsp. paprika
3/4	tsp. salt
	oil for frying, heated to 375°
	lemon wedges and parsley for garnish

Dip the fish into the combined egg and milk, then coat with a mixture of out flour, mustard, baking powder, paprika and salt. Fry in oil for about 3 minutes per side, or until crisp and golden brown, turning only once. Drain on absorbent paper. Garnish with lemon slices and parsley, if desired.

*To make ground oat flour: Place 1¼ cups of uncooked quick or old-fashioned oats, in a blender or food processor. Cover and blend for about 60 seconds. Store in a tightly covered container in a cool dry place for up to 6 months. Use for baking, breading, thickening, or dredging and browning. When using for baking, substitute up to, but not more than, ⅓ of the oat flour with all-purpose flour.

Harvey Bolstad
Gilman, Wisconsin

BAKED FISH FILLETS

  2   lbs. any kind of fresh fish fillets
 ½ tsp. paprika
  3   T. lemon juice
      salt
      pepper
  2   T. butter or margarine
  2   T. flour
  1   T. dry mustard
  1   cup milk
 ½ cup buttered bread crumbs
  1   T. chopped fresh parsley

Cut the fillets into serving pieces. Place in a greased shallow baking dish and sprinkle with paprika, lemon juice, and salt and pepper to your taste. Make a white sauce by melting the butter in a saucepan; stir in flour and mustard, blend in milk, and cook until thickened, stirring constantly. Pour sauce over the fillets. Sprinkle the bread crumbs and parsley over the fish, and bake at 350° for 30-35 minutes.

Donald R. Payjack
Calgary, Alberta

FISH SUPREME

  2   lbs. fish fillets, any kind
  2   cups Italian bread crumbs
  2   cups grated Parmesan cheese
  1   tsp. garlic powder
  1   tsp. pepper
  1   lb. melted butter or margarine
      paprika

Combine the bread crumbs, cheese, garlic and pepper. Wet the fish and toss in crumbs. Place the fish in a pan; pour the butter over it and shake paprika over it. Bake at 350° for 30 minutes.

Lenny Gale
Nashua, New Hampshire

FRIED FISH

1	fish fillets
	salt
	pepper
	peanut oil
1-2	eggs
1-2	T. water
	potato flakes

Put ¼ inch of peanut oil in the bottom of an electric skillet and set the temperature to 375-400°. Dry both sides of the fillets on paper towels, and then salt and pepper them. Thoroughly mix the eggs and water, dip each fillet in the mix and then drop it in the potato flakes. Shake in a bag to coat each fillet. Cook in the hot peanut oil until golden brown on each side.

Everett E. Rowland
Estill Springs, Tennessee

SMOKED FISH

	fish
2	quarts water
½-¾	cup salt
½	cup brown sugar
¼	cup lemon juice
1	round tsp. garlic powder
1	round tsp. onion powder

Mix together all of the ingredients, except the fish, to form the brine. Cut the fish into chunks and soak in the brine overnight. Take the fish out and rinse in cool water then let it air dry for 1 hour. Smoke in a wet smoker for 2½ hours using the juice from the brine. Or, smoke dry for 4½-5 hours.

Kenneth M. Taylor
Fallon, Nevada

ANY FISH BROILED OR FRIED

fish fillets
$\frac{1}{2}$ cup yellow cornmeal
$\frac{1}{2}$ cup flour
$\frac{1}{2}$ tsp. salt
$\frac{1}{2}$ tsp. black pepper
$\frac{1}{2}$ tsp. ground nutmeg
olive oil for frying

Shake the fish in a bag with all of the dry ingredients, then fry in the oil.

Kenneth D. Kennedy
Middletown, California

BAKED FILLETS

fresh fillets
processed cheese (mild colby, etc.), shredded
green peppers, chopped
onions, chopped
lemon juice

Place the fillets on a cookie sheet and spread the cheese on them. Put the green pepper and onions over the cheese. Bake for 20 minutes at 350°. Squeeze on drops of lemon juice. This fish can be served as a main course or an appetizer.

Duane Nayrocker
Wabash, Indiana

CAMP FISH

	fish		pepper
2	cups potato flakes		eggs, beaten
3	T. flour		oil for frying
	salt		

Mix the dry ingredients together in a bag. Fillet the fish, dip it in the egg, and then into the potato flake mixture. Fry in hot oil until done.

William S. Richards
Silver Bay, Minnesota

DON'S SUPER FISH BAKE

2   lbs. boneless fish fillets
2   medium potatoes, sliced thin
1   medium onion, sliced thin
1   8-oz. package of frozen creamed spinach
1   8-oz. package of frozen chopped broccoli
    Swiss cheese, grated or sliced thin

Sauce:
1   small can of evaporated milk
1   can of cream of mushroom soup
$1/2$ cup white wine
$1/8$ tsp. garlic powder
$1/4$ tsp. dried basil
$1/4$ tsp. black pepper

Preheat the oven to 350°. Mix the sauce ingredients in a bowl. Layer the bottom of a baking dish with $1/3$ of the sauce. Then layer with half potatoes, fish fillets, and onion, all of the spinach, and another $1/3$ of the sauce. Repeat layers using the broccoli in place of spinach. Top with Swiss cheese. Bake for 1 hour.

Donald Krenson
Miami, Florida

BAKED FILLET OF FISH

    6   fish fillets
    2   T. olive oil
        salt
        pepper
  1-2   tsp. seafood seasoning
        juice of 2 fresh lemons
    2   fresh tomatoes, cut into wedges
    1   green pepper, thinly sliced
  2-3   stems of fresh basil

Put the olive oil in a baking pan and lay the fish fillets over top. Salt and pepper them to taste, and add the seafood seasoning. Drizzle the lemon juice over the top. Spread the tomato wedges and green pepper slices over the top. Add the fresh basil.

Bake at 375° for 30 minutes. Drain off some of the liquid and broil for 5 minutes.

Mrs. Raymond D. Weikel
Hatboro, Pennsylvania

CAMPFIRE FISH DINNER

    1   fresh fish
    2   slices of bacon
    1   potato
    1   onion
        seasoning to taste

Clean the fish and lay out on piece of aluminum foil that is large enough to wrap the fish. Place a strip of bacon on the foil and put fish on the bacon. Put slices of potato and onion on the fish and top with another slice of bacon. Season to taste, seal fish in foil, and cook in the coals of a campfire for about 20 minutes.

Scott Green
Salt Lake City, Utah

FISH SALAD

1¼ lbs. fresh fish (steaks or fillets), thawed and rinsed
    Cajun spice mix
  1 stalk celery with leaves, chopped
 ¼ large or ½ medium red or green bell pepper
 ½ medium onion, chopped
 ½ cup mayonnaise
  1 hot pepper, seeded and chopped fine (optional)

Rinse the fish and pat dry. Place the fish in an even layer on a sheet of foil large enough to enclose it. Sprinkle the fish with the Cajun spice to taste. Wrap the fish in the foil and steam on a rack over boiling water for 12-15 minutes until done. Remove from the heat.

Place the foil package on a plate in the refrigerator until cooled. When chilled, remove the fish and flake it into a bowl. Mix with the other ingredients. Serve in sandwiches or on crackers.

Another serving suggestion: Core, clean and stuff peppers or tomatoes with the salad.

Note: The steaming was done on a raised wire rack in a covered frying pan. The steaming time may vary if other methods are used.

Fred Stopper
Philadelphia, Pennsylvania

FAVORITE FISH RECIPE

4-6 fish fillets, with all bones removed
2 cups finely crumbled crackers
2 cups grated Parmesan cheese (fresh is best)
1/2 cup butter or margarine

Mix the crackers and the cheese. Melt the butter or the margarine and brush it on both sides of the fish fillets. Roll the fish in the cracker/cheese mixture. Place the fish on a cookie sheet and bake in a 350° oven for 10 minutes. The cooking time will vary depending upon the thickness of the fillets. Turn on the broiler for the last 2 minutes of cooking time for a crunchy outside. Serve with your favorite condiments and side dishes.

Bret H. Merchant
Seabrook, Texas

FISH DELITE

Fish fillets, cut into serving size pieces
1 cup yellow cornmeal
1 cup flour
sprinkle of dried thyme
touch of garlic salt
1 T. monosodium glutamate
1 dash of paprika
1 sprinkle of pepper
1/2 cup finely ground bacon bits
oil for frying

Mix all of the ingredients together (except the fish and the oil) and bread the damp fish with the mixture. Cook the fish in the oil until brown and serve while it is still hot. This is a real treat when applied to walleye, perch, crappie or bluegill. 1½ pounds of this breading is enough for 6 pounds of fish.

Loren Gillespie
Tremont, Illinois

NEVADA PICKLED FISH

1 quart of fish,
  skinned, boned
  and cut into
  small pieces
⅝ cup 10 T. non-
  iodized salt
  white vinegar
  onion slices
  sugar
  pickling spices

Kenneth M. Taylor

Place the cut-up fish loosely in a jar. Add the salt and cover the fish with white vinegar. Let that stand for 5 days in the refrigerator.

Remove the fish pieces and wash them in cold water. Let them stand in clear, cold water for ½ hour. Then pack the fish loosely in jars again. Add raw, sliced onions to each jar. Cover the fish with a cold solution that is 2 parts white vinegar to 1 part sugar. Add whole pickling spices (about one box to each 2 quarts of vinegar used).

Do not seal the jars tightly. Keep them cool in the refrigerator. You can start eating them in a couple of days.

Kenneth M. Taylor
Fallon, Nevada

FRIED CAMPING FISH

	any freshwater fish can be used
1¹/₂	cups yellow cornmeal
³/₄	cup self-rising flour
1	cup buttermilk or sweet milk
2-3	green onions, chopped fine
	cayenne pepper
	salt (optional)
1-2	eggs
	real lemon juice
	oil for frying

Combine all of the ingredients, except the fish and the oil. Dip the fish in this batter and fry in oil until brown. Serve with hush puppies.

Roy Gazaway
Louisville, Missouri

OVEN-FRIED FISH

1	lb. of your favorite fish fillets
¹/₂	cup crushed cornflakes
¹/₂	tsp. celery salt
¹/₈	tsp. onion powder
¹/₈	tsp. paprika
	dash of pepper
1	T. skim milk

Combine all of the dry ingredients. Dip the fish in the milk and then roll in the corn flake mixture. Place the fish in a baking pan and cook in a preheated 350° oven for 25 minutes, or until brown.

Maria & Walter Northway, Jr.
Pequot Lakes, Minnesota

MY WIFE'S FAMOUS PICKLED FISH

1   quart fish fillets
1   cup salt
4   cups water
    white vinegar

For brine:
2   cups white vinegar
1   cup white port wine
1   cup sugar
1   T. pickling spices
    onion, slices
    lemon, slices

Cut the fish into strips. Mix the salt and water in a large container and soak the fish in this solution for 24 hours. Drain and rinse well with cold water. Put then fish back into the container and cover with white vinegar. Soak the fish for 48 hours, then drain the vinegar off but do not rinse.

To make the brine: Combine the 2 cups vinegar, port wine, sugar and pickling spices. Simmer for a few minutes and then remove spices. Cool the brine. In a large bucket (ice cream buckets work well), arrange the fish in layers with generous amounts of sliced onion and a few slices of lemon. Pour the cooled brine over the fish. Cover and refrigerate for at least 2 weeks.

Myron Lange
Augusta, Wisconsin

Pickled Fish and Red Peppers

3-4 quarts fish
      white vinegar
      water
      sliced onions
½   cup wine
      juice of ½ lemon

Brine:

2   cups white vinegar
1 ¾ cups sugar
4   bay leaves
5   whole cloves
1   tsp. whole allspice
2   tsp. mustard seed
4   red peppers, chopped

Clean fish and cut into small pieces. Put fish in salt brine, about 1½ cups pickling salt to 3-4 cups cold water. Let stand 48 hours in refrigerator. Drain and rinse thoroughly with cold water. Add enough white vinegar to cover and let stand in refrigerator 24 hours or longer. The vinegar will dissolve any bones you miss. Drain.

Add onion slices to taste, the lemon juice, and the wine. Mix. Combine the brine ingredients, boil for 5 minutes, then cool. Pour brine over fish, mix, let stand. Pack fish in clean jars, fill with brine and seal. Refrigerate for 1 week, and fish will be ready to eat.

James Roy Marschel, Sr.
Buffalo, Minnesota

STOKES' PICKLED FISH

3-4 lbs. fish fillets, cut into bite-size pieces
good quality distilled white vinegar (at least 5% acetic acid)

Brine:

6 cups soft water
1 cup pickling salt

Pickling Solution:

1 cup soft water
½ cup sugar (brown or white)
2 cups vinegar
2 T. pickling spices
4 whole cloves
4 T. pimiento slices
1 medium onion, sliced
3 drops hot pepper sauce (optional)

Put the fish into a glass bowl, cover with the brine, and refrigerate overnight (about 12 hours). Remove the fish from the brine and rinse. Place the fish back in a clean bowl and cover with the distilled white vinegar. Cover the bowl and refrigerate overnight. Remove the fish from the vinegar and rinse.

To make the pickling solution: Mix all of the ingredients together in a saucepan. Bring to a boil, reduce the heat and simmer for 15 minutes. Cool to room temperature before pouring onto the fish.

Place the fish in pint jars, packing it in a bit. Cover the fish completely with the pickling solution. Place lids on the jars and refrigerate for 5 days. Shake the jars periodically to ensure that the pickling solution reaches all the fish.

David Stokes
Duluth, Minnesota

LEMON PICKLED FISH

6	quarts fish, cut to desired size
2	quarts cider vinegar
2½	cups canning salt
2	quarts white vinegar
1	bay leaf
½	small box of pickling spice
5	cups white sugar
½	cup olive oil
3	onions, thinly sliced
2	lemons, thinly sliced

Mix the fish, cidar vinegar and salt in glass or plastic bowl, and refrigerate for 6 days, stirring daily. Drain and wash 3-4 times, and then drain well. Boil the remaining ingredients (except the onions and lemons) together and then cool. Place the fish pieces in jars and pour the cooled mixture over the fish. Add the onions and lemons to the jars.

Note: I remove the lemon slices after a few days as the lemon flavor gets too strong. The fish can be eaten after 2 days, but the longer you can wait, the better it tastes.

Cam Powers
Nashua, Iowa

POACHED FISH WITH CUCUMBER SAUCE

4-6 lbs. fish fillets   2 bay leaves
  2 medium onions, sliced   2 tsp. salt
  6 slices of onion   4 peppercorns
  6 sprigs of parsley

In two 12 inch skillets, heat 1½ inch of water to boiling and divide all ingredients, except the fish, evenly between the 2 pans. Add the fish in a single layer and cover. Simmer for 6-8 minutes, or until the fish flakes easily. Remove the fish to a serving platter and pour cucumber sauce (recipe below)over the top.

CUCUMBER SAUCE

¼ cup shortening
2 T. flour
2 cups milk
3 egg yolks, slightly beaten
1 cucumber, pared, seeded and diced
1 can shrimp, rinsed, drained and chopped
1 tsp. salt
¼ tsp. ground nutmeg
⅛ tsp. pepper

Melt the shortening in a medium saucepan. Blend in the flour. Cook over low heat, stirring until the mixture is smooth and bubbly. Remove from the heat. Stir in the milk. Heat to boiling, stirring constantly. Boil and stir for 1 minute. Remove from the heat.

Stir at least half of the hot mixture into the egg yolks. Then slowly blend the egg mixture into the remaining hot mixture. Boil and stir for 1 minute. Stir in the remaining ingredients and heat through. Pour over fish and serve.

David Stokes
Duluth, Minnesota

FISH JERKY

$^3/_8$" strips
4   tsp. salt
$^1/_4$ tsp. pepper
2   tsp. onion powder
$^1/_2$ tsp. garlic powder
2   T. parsley flakes, crushed
$^1/_2$ cup lemon juice
2   lbs. fish (I like trout and walleye best), sliced into

Combine all of the ingredients, except the fish. Layer the fish in a shallow container, coating each layer with the combined ingredients. Cover tightly and marinate overnight in the refrigerator. Put the strips in a food dehydrator and dry until fish feels firm, dry and tough, but not crumbly. It should take 10-24 hours, depending on the power of your dehydrator.

James Hyer McKechnie
Shelby, Montana

LEMON PEPPER CATCH OF THE DAY

4   fish fillets perch
1   large onion, sliced
      into rings
¼   cup melted butter
1   T. parsley flakes
      (can also use fresh
      parsley)
½   cup cornmeal
1   T. lemon pepper
½   cup bread crumbs
1   egg
1   T. water

Beat the egg and the water together. Combine the cornmeal, lemon pepper, and bread crumbs. Dip the fillets into the egg and then into the bread crumbs to coat on both sides. Place the fillets in a single layer in a baking dish. Spread the onions over the top. Sprinkle parsley and butter over them all. Bake at 350° for 45 minutes.

Joseph W. Puchalski

Joseph W. Puchalski
Newburgh, New York

INDEX

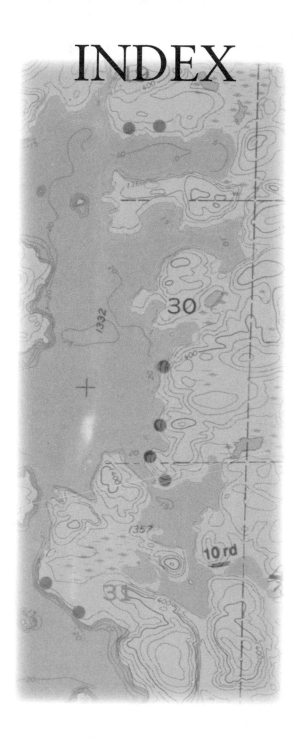